THE LETTER

THE LETTER

A memoir

JAMUNA ADVANI

PARTRIDGE
A Penguin Random House Company

To order additional copies of this book, contact
Partridge India
000 800 10062 62
orders.india@partridgepublishing.com

www.partridgepublishing.com/india

Acknowledgement

The journey of writing this book has been a long one, from gathering my memories of childhood days to selecting the many daily events I recorded in my journal after moving from India to Canada and then to the US. I am so thankful to all my children and friends for their encouraging words and for helping me sustain my determination.

I am especially grateful and indebted to my editor Ms. Sheila Bender for her contribution of time and energy while editing my book. Also thanks to Mr. Kapil Arambam for the cover design.

DEDICATION

This book is in honor of my Grandmother Rajkumari Sanachaubi Devi, a caring and loving person who was always ready to do whatever she could help all of us whenever we needed her. Because of her far-sighted vision for future, I have my loving brothers and their kids to whom I can proudly say I have a place to go back home.

May this record of our ancestors help future generations understand their origin and our Manipuri Meitei roots.

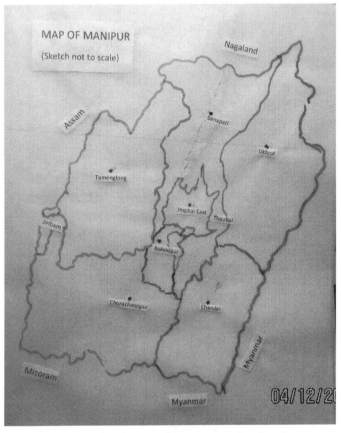

Figure 1 a sketch map of Manipur and its borders

Above is my rough sketch of Manipur state showing the nine districts of Manipur. Jiribam is under Imphal West.

California
October 22, 2013

Dear Gojen,

 I am confident that you're the nephew who will take a keen interest in reading my letters about my life and our family. Although your cousins may not at this moment feel like learning more about where they came from, I believe the subject will come up someday and I hope you will share my letters.

 On September 17, 1994 I wrote a journal entry about leaving India on my way to Canada that I will share here, and I shall be writing later on with stories of growing up in Jiribam alongside of journal entries about other days. First I want you to know that I have often relied on this quote to help me stir up my course: "Let your passions be the reasons for your existence and your successes the product of your persistence."

 First, a poem I wrote on a cloudy day inspired by the quote I hold dear:

A Pen in My Hand

I channel the stream of my journal
On these blank pages
With my intentions intact accompanied by
Inborn instincts and aspirations.

To unfold the present and the past
Holding the light of hope with a desire
To illumine the crevices of the blurred future
I shall let this pen lift my spirit
Above the clouds of doubt.

Journal Entry
September 17, 1994

This part of my life is indeed inscribed in the leaves of my memory tree and can never be erased. We have been given official immigration to Canada and my journey starts today. I am ready to face an unknown future in a new country leaving behind my friends and family in India.

I am on my way to Toronto with a stopover at Heathrow International Airport, London while my son Jibesh is scheduled to meet me on the same flight at Heathrow airport after visiting his friend in Ireland. My husband Rup is still in India as he has to complete some work before he joins us in Canada.

The British Airways Boeing 747 flight is on time. After nearly ten hours it landed smoothly and now I must wait for the next connection to Toronto. As soon as we are allowed to get out of the aircraft, I proceed hurriedly to that gate. I'm slightly overweight for my height of 5'2", but I am quite active and walk fast even though I have more than four hours before my next flight. And, of course, I am anxious to see Jibesh.

Before my departure from India I colored my hair brown and cut it into a chin length bob at Millie's Salon, Chittaranjan Park, New Delhi. The black sandals I wear now are from Bata Shoe store and are comfortable during long flights. Wearing black corduroy pants and a cotton printed blouse with my gray cardigan, its sleeves wrapped around my neck, I have a black leather purse on my shoulder and pull my carryon bag toward my gate, # 66. I am relieved when I find it. At peace and relaxed with time to spare, I turn toward the café nearby for a cup of coffee. While I wait for Jibesh to arrive, I keep myself occupied watching people and looking at the rows of shops. As the time for boarding approaches and there is no sign of my son, I feel a pinch of nervousness and my heart starts pumping faster and faster. I wait among all the passengers who are boarding the aircraft. Where is Jibesh? Will he appear soon? Now all the passengers have boarded. Anxiety is blowing all over me. As I proceed toward the aircraft, frustration and anger stir up in me and I start blaming my husband Rup for allowing him to go ahead just to see his girlfriend. Worries fill me up to my neck at the thought of facing immigration all alone in Toronto. Reluctantly, I board the aircraft and take my seat. Now the fact settles in me that I will have to face the immigration officer at Pearson International Airport all alone. I need to sum up my courage and ready for it.

I shall continue to write more about my childhood days and later part of my life. I send lots of love to you and your family.

Yours lovingly,
Ine

*   *   *

Etobicoke, Ontario, Canada
March 3, 1995

Dear Gojen,

I write today regarding an incident which happened in
Jiribam when I was about 9 years old. It is sort of a confession
about something I haven't told to anyone so far. It happened just
after all my cousins left for Imphal at the end of WWll. I hope
you will find it a bit amusing.

That afternoon I finished my studies for the day and came
out of the house into the front yard to swing under the grapefruit
tree. I still remember the rhythm of the swing and the pampering
of the breeze on my face. It was indeed a time to forget about
everything including my worries about math. I kept the gate
open to a view of the main entrance to our house in case my
grandmother or mother tried to look out for me

On my swing, I shifted my attention when I saw a man
approach our house. I was surprised by his sudden appearance.
I recognized him as he used to visit my father quite often. I
called him "Khura," which means uncle. He didn't talk to me
or say anything but went straight to our house and knocked on
the front door. We were not supposed to call by name to any
one older. We had to oblige to show respect. Khura maintained
his patience while still waiting for someone to open the door.
I stopped swinging and watched him. After some time my
grandmother, my mother's mother, Sanachaubi, opened the door
and came out. She too looked surprised to see Khura Chauba.
She greeted him and offered a mura (a stool made of cane)

"Come and sitdown." She signaled him to take the stool.
"Anything I can do for you?" People from the neighboring

villages often came to my father for advice and help in legal matters.

"I am all right; I come here to deliver news about your son-in-law." He answered.

"Is he all right? What's happened?"

He mumbled something to my grandmother Sanachaubi. I could see my grandmother's expression change but I couldn't tell if she was worried or angry. After few seconds there was some conversation. Although I couldn't hear what they were talking about, I imagined this conversation was not good one. Khura Chauba got up and said something more and left. He seemed to be in a hurry, rushing toward the front gate and walking away as fast as he could, maybe to his home at Kalinagar village. Grandmother stood deep in thought, watching him go. There was some concern I could see on her face. Then she turned toward me.

"Jamuna come inside, quick." She gave me a signal to go inside.

Though I wanted to stay longer on my swing, my inquisitive mind and the urgency in her voice made me disengage from the swing and walk to find out what had just happened. Maybe something serious happened, I thought to myself. By the time I reached the verandah my grandmother was already inside and I saw her talking to my mother. It was in a very serious tone. As I entered they both looked at me and in their eyes I could sense something was wrong. "What's happened? What did Khura say?"

My mother's face was turned away from me and she didn't try to look at me, maybe trying to hide tears.

"Your father has eloped with Kunjo," was my grandmother's response. I could not believe it, because Kunjo was a married woman and living with her husband at the neighboring village Kalinagar. We heard the rumor of their affair but I did not think she would elope with my father. That woman was crazy,

I thought. It was as if we were trapped inside the whirlpool of a storm.

"Are you sure?" I just couldn't believe it. But it was hope against hope. We had to acknowledge it. As anxiety and curiosity combined, I couldn't help but asked, "Where are they now?

"At Lakhipur, at your aunt Pashot's place." My grandmother replied in a pensive mood. My mother kept quiet and did not utter a single word.

My father and Kunjo must have walked 10 miles from Jiribam to reach Aunt Pashot's place in Lakhipur village in Cachar. There the hilly road was not motorable in those days.

Father came back after three days and continued to work at his office as if nothing had happened. It was during the early forties; people working in the civil administrative office as well as other departments were like VIPs and the poor villagers couldn't say anything publically, only whisper among themselves. My mother and grandmother had to accept my father's new wife. What else could they do? Women were not educated and depended on their husbands for their living. Every Saturday father went to his new wife and came back on Sunday. This routine went on for a month. My father looked exhausted walking ten miles on the hilly path from Jiribam to Lakhipur and back every weekend. My grandmother could see the strain in his face and at the same time the heavy financial strain. She finally gave father a suggestion which he embraced immediately. The plan was to build a cottage in the backyard between our quarter and the kitchen on the northern side, an open space available at that time. The idea seemed to be a favorable one and immediately father started collecting materials for the construction.

My father being an all rounder, knew how to build the cottage, and completed it without anybody's help within three months, with no drainage system, no running water and also no electricity. Four months since the elopement, Kunjo was welcomed to our house and allotted the new cottage. Everything went on normally. Our house was like before and there was no tension as there had been during their affair. Cooking was done by my mother except when she had her period. Then my grandmother took a turn. Kunjo was not allowed to enter the cooking area in the kitchen because she was a divorcee and also not from high a caste as Grandmother, who was an honored lady in her society. I remember how she was provided front row seating at social events, just like those of the Brahmin caste, who were considered the very highest rank in the hierarchy of the caste system.

Kunjo usually did other household chores such as washing clothes and utensils and pounding rice from husks while mother did the cooking and helped Kunjo in the pounding of rice and other household chores.

My mother (I call her Ima) was a saintly woman; father and she were in opposite poles. But none of the women before or after my mother could live with Father long enough. So mother was the only one who looked after him till the end.

I was around nine years of age when father expressed his desire to have a son for the family. Even though my mother was in her late twenties only, she had not conceived even when I was 9 years old. So everyone started doubting that my mother would give birth to another child. But he didn't realize that Kunjo had not begot a child with her previous husband and since she was in her late thirties, it was doubtful that she would have one now.

Three months passed since Kunjo had come into our house. One fine day Grandmother was in a good mood, her face covered with layers of excitement. She called me inside our room as if she had just found a fortune. I shut my book and rose from the mat. She waited for me holding a package in her hand.

She pulled out a paper and gave it to me to read. I found it very difficult to understand. "Read again carefully till the end and we have to follow the instructions," she insisted. I started reading again slowly.

I had goose bumps. "No, I can't. I don't think I can do it!" I almost shouted.

She placed her index finger on her lips, a signal to make me quiet.

"We have to follow all the instructions. And we have to be very careful. No one should know." She said.

I had to obey her.

I managed to memorize the mantra written on that piece of paper. It was not an easy one as the words were in some sort of ancient language used by our ancestors. Someone in the village gave Grandmother the name of the sorcerer and she spent money for it. In this deal, Grandmother and I were the only ones involved. My mother would not be a part of this. I think I was quite smart for my age. It was crucial moment for us that things should happen as we wanted. We let my mother remain as saintly as she was. Grandmother made me believe that we had to follow this path for the welfare of the family.

Three days passed, and nothing happened as Kunjo was at home, never gone from the house. Finally on the 4th day she was all dressed, wearing her favorite cream colored phanek (skirt) and a light green colored cotton shawl. She plucked a champa (leihau) flower from the tree in our front yard. The pink flower, the size of a small finger in the shape of a tulip hung on her right side in a few strands of her hair. The champa flower gave off a heavenly scent.

I spoke, trying to be casual. "Imaton (younger mother), oh such a sweet fragrance, and you look so beautiful; where are you going?"

She smiled, "To Kali temple and then to meet my friend at Kalinagar."

"Oh! You will be gone for some time I guess."

"Yes, I'll be back as soon as I finish my work and after meeting my friend. I'll start pounding the rice after I come back." She told me to convey the message to my mom and grandma. She headed toward the gate walking on the street leading to the Kali Temple.

My mother was in the kitchen and Grandma was in the loom weaving. It was around 12 noon when she left after finishing lunch and all the dishes were done. Father was already at work and hence no one else was around. Now that Kunjo was out of the house we could proceed with our plan. It was perfect weather during that time in Jiribam. We didn't experience the cold winter like that in Imphal town or any other part of Northern India. Jiribam was pleasant for a few weeks in winter and then scorching again in the months that followed.

My mother went to her room after her cooking and cleaning of her kitchen. My grandmother had been keeping her eye on me and now she and I nodded in agreement. She stopped weaving and came out to see if Kunjo was far enough away for us to take the risk. She gave me the packet, which was kept hidden under her roll of threads near the loom. I opened it a little bit to see if those I saw before were still inside. I knew what was to be done.

Grandma waited outside on the verandah to watch in case Kunjo turned back to come to her room. I waited for my grandmother's signal. Finally she gave it. I proceeded toward Kunjo's room. Even though I knew it was now safe, my heart beat was going up as I entered her bedroom.

The bed was neatly arranged with a light green sheet and the pillows covered with embroidered white cases. Everything was kept in its place. The sweet pleasant aroma of champa flowers, which she kept near her bed, filled the room. My admiration of her was growing. Suddenly, I remembered that I had to complete my mission fast. I took out the seven pieces of broomstick Grandma had kept hidden, and recited the mantra I'd learned three times over them. Holding them with my right hand, I swept the bed from the middle toward the opposite directions. After repeating the action three times and completing the ritual, I came out as fast as possible with the packet intact with the mantra paper inside. My grandmother, her face still toward the road stood watching for Kunjo, looked relieved when she saw me coming out of the room.

"You did a good job." She was overjoyed with my performance. Everything went smoothly. Our plan was to repeat and follow the same procedure wherever Kunjo went out of the house. We had been lucky as she went regularly to the temple and also to meet her friend. We continued the same ritual as directed by the sorcerer. In two months, we had completed the ritual at least ten times. I was no longer nervous as I was on the first day. And my grandmother made sure that everything went smoothly.

After four months, my grandmother said, "There seems to be some change."

"What change?" I was curious.

"Your father is not very much interested in going to her."

"Oh, is it so? I questioned.

"See, he is not going to her room as often as he used to be."

Maybe she is right and our mantra is working and getting the result, I thought to myself. By the end of the fifth month Kunjo looked quite depressed and miserable. I wonder what happened between her and my father. One fine morning, she left for her parents' home in Cachar. We were not sure if she was going to come back as my father never talked about her. Maybe the sorcerer's magic had worked. A few days after Kunjo's departure, I heard my grandmother talking to her friend Leiriksana, who visited our house occasionally.

"Is she coming back?" Leiriksana asked my grandmother about Kunjo as she had the last time she visited our house.

"I guess it is unlikely," my grandmother replied. "I'm looking for a girl for my son-in-law." The lady looked surprised. Then *as realization dawned on her that my grandmother was serious she responded, "Well I'll see if there is a suitable match for him, someone who can give a son." This was an understanding among all the people concerned. A son is needed for the family's name to continue. I kept asking myself why a girl cannot be an asset to the family.*

The rest of the story I shall be writing to you soon.

Yours lovingly,
Ine

*   *   *

Journal Entry
Toronto, Ontario Canada
September 19, 1994

After my arrival at Pearson International airport, Toronto, all wrapped up in my worries I proceed toward the immigration. I hand over my papers to the immigration officer. The officer is Canadian; he looks quite the friendly type and he goes through all the documents while I look at him expectantly hoping he lets me pass through soon. Then anxious to meet my daughter and son-in-law who are supposed to be waiting for me, I continue waiting expentantly. Instead, he makes me go to another room and tells me to wait there. Wrapped up in my nervousness, I start chanting God's name silently.

The officer comes back after a few minutes and tells me, "The main applicant is your husband; he needs to be here." I look at him in disbelief.

"We had requested to change the main applicant to be me instead of Rup Advani, and it was done and cleared in India," I respond.

"We have already sent a fax and we shall wait for the confirmation reply from our office in India." I feel helpless. What else to do but just wait with all of my wild imaginings filling my brain. The officer looks kind and very helpful, and is courteous; he doesn't make me feel unwelcome.

So I am now drowned completely in my anxiety. I start blaming my husband for letting me handle all of these problems all alone; over and above I am annoyed at my son for missing his flight. After two hours or so I am cleared and I become an official resident of Canada. Now I see a clear sky with bright sunshine as I see my daughter and son-in-law outside. I learn that my son Jibesh has sent a message that he missed the flight from Ireland and will be reaching Canada four hours later.

When I see my son with his luggage tagging along I thank God that there is new hope for the future and we shall go through together. Jibesh is only the one on whom I now depend. My daughter is leaving for Brazil with her husband in two days and hence they have vacated their apartment and now living in a weekly rental. They are waiting for our arrival before they leave for Brazil.

Jibesh drives them to Montreal to catch their flight to Brazil. That night I stay alone at the weekly rental room. It is the scariest night in my life. Overcrowded with our suitcases, the room hardly has space to walk around. As the darkness approached and the door locked and double checked, I try to sleep but with no result. I stay awake thinking of the future. I hear a clicking sound of a key through my room's key hole. I look at my watch; it is around 1:30 am. There is no phone in the room (there were no cell phones in those days), so that

I can contact someone. I feel so helpless and try to stop my breathing in case if someone is there whoever he is will not hear me. Luckily, after few trials the clicking noise stops. May be he is drunk and doesn't remember his room number. And I take a deep breath and exhale out the fear.

Impatiently Indulgent

I face the unsuspecting problems
That have stumbled me along life's pavement.

I cannot erase those,
Even wishing to start all over again.
It's too late to even to think about it.

Luckily, we can get an apartment at the Stevenson Court by the week's end. My son and I will be in the one bedroom apartment until we get a proper place and start our business. Life here is tough now, all work and worry until things settle down.

* * *

Etobicoke, Ontario Canada
February 10, 1995

My Dear Gojen,

Today I want to tell you about one of those memories I have treasured and kept with me until this day. It is of an incident that happened while Pabun (my dad) was tutoring me in math.

I was about 7 years old and it was during winter of 1942. I remember that because the kitchen garden in our huge backyard was full of mustard leaves and peas growing in luxuriant green. How I enjoyed plucking those tender green peas and popping them in my mouth. That Sunday morning in particular, Pabung wanted to teach me how to solve a simple math problem. I couldn't avoid it. We sat on the mat spread on the floor of our back verandah, basking in the winter's pleasant warm sunshine. He wanted me to practice reading Manipuri and English too. I enjoyed reading both. But the moment he mentioned math, I dreaded and wanted to hide somewhere he couldn't find me. I could see the wooden ruler lying near us and a math problem coming up. His patience draining away, I had to plan my strategy. That day I decided I'd not let him get me with that ruler on my back. I looked sideways and saw him reaching for that ruler. I did something I never did before. I surprised him as I stood up suddenly and ran away toward the backyard where my mother was busy plucking some vegetables.

"Ima, Ima, please hide me," I shouted. My mom stood up wondering what was happening. Still holding her basket full of mustard leaves and cilantro along with some green peppers and peas, she looked at me. Mother, always a quiet subdued and kind person, that day changed completely to protect her daughter like a lioness protecting her pups. She dropped her basket and extended her arms to guard me and hide me under the shawl she wore.

"Enough, enough," Mom uttered forcefully when he approached to get me.

Pabung, with the wooden ruler in his hand, tried to catch me but my fast shifting movement behind my mother, whose arms extended to guard me, brought me into a safety zone.

Maybe he found my running away and hiding behind my mother's shawl amusing. He finally changed his mind and left us alone. The memory of that day's incident remained with me forever and mathematics is a subject I abhor to this day. Not having a school in Jiribam, a rural and remote place, my destiny was carved by my father's tutoring effort. How I wished my mom or grandmother could take his place. As my father had a high I Q, he could not imagine that I didn't have the abilities to grasp the math the way he wanted of me.

But still I feel, if he had more patience with me and my IQ, I could have loved math as much as any other subject. When father initiated to establish a school in Jiribam, from elementary to sixth grade, I was overwhelmed with joy.

As the only child till I was twelve, I was pampered and protected by all, especially my grandmother. After the school started in Jiribam one particular teacher was accommodated in one of the rooms in our quarter. I think his name was Nanda Kishor. He was given the responsibility for tutoring me while he worked for the school as one of the teachers. Those teachers were from Cachar district of the neighboring state of Assam in North East India. Even though I continued to pass the math, I could never develop any interest in this subject while I loved literature and other subjects. The new chapter of my life started as we had to move to Imphal after I finished middle school. Luckily father got transferred to Imphal after 18 years' posting in Jiribam. I believe it was some sort of exile for him, because of his bad circle of friends involved in gambling and thus dwindling away the family wealth. I shall write you more in my next letter. Bye now. Before ending my letter I attach the following entries from my journal about when I started my life in Canada and USA.

Yours lovingly,
Ine

* * *

Journal Entry
Toronto, 1995

I am trying to get a job while planning to take a test so that I can work as a nurse since I have a nursing degree from the University of Delhi. I have not worked since the birth of my second daughter Shobha in 1964. My son's degree from Kolkata University is not recognized in Canada. To my surprise he has no interest in further studies and while looking for something to do which suits him, he joins his friend in the construction business for the time being.

At the same time, enticed by business advertisements and brochures, I spend quite a few bucks and find myself entangled with the illusion of AMWAY. Even though some achieve their goal, it is not an easy one to reach. I drop out as soon as I realize it is beyond my capacity. Later I get job as a caregiver in a nursing facility while still studying for the test so I can resume my nursing career. But one day on TV news I hear about the firing of nursing staff, and I drop my intention of pursuing my nursing career into the dust bin. I never try to take any advice from others; neither do I look around at fellow nurses from whom I can take some advice. That's the mistake I have made and I regret now. I just continue working at the nursing care facility in Toronto for some time.

Rup comes and joins us in Toronto. He and our son are planning to start some business. But he wants to start only after he settles a work problem that he is facing back home. The case has been going on for some time and he needs to settle everything with the bank before he decides to launch some plan he has in his mind. Presently he stays with our son while I stay in the nursing faculty as I am supposed to be there for 24 hours. Since the facility doesn't give enough time to be away, I decide to quit my job. I join a cosmetology class at the Community College. It is very interesting and I really like it.

Journal Entry
Toronto, Ontario
July 2, 1995

By this time after almost one year, my daughter Lata and her husband Louie come back from Brazil as she is expecting her first baby and she wants to give birth in Canada. They have sold their business to return to Canada. They are in an apartment near our place at Etobicoke. Her baby is due in October and she is taking care of herself and the baby as it is her first pregnancy at the age of 34. Her husband Louie has two kids from the previous marriage. My husband's plan to start a business is not encouraged by my family in Canada. In fact, we have come to Canada because my son wants to be here and he could come only if parents immigrated hence we had to apply ourselves for his sake. Having postponed the idea of starting a business, Rup decides to go back to India after six months on August 20, 1995. He wants to settle the issues with the bank and come back to Canada permanently.

The uneasy feeling inside me tells me something is not right and the uncertainty of our plan makes me feel insecure; his going away only shows me a dark and obscure future. My intuition most of the time comes out right.

He walks slowly away toward the gate after he checks his luggage and gets his boarding pass and a part of me is missing. I try to hide my tears from my daughter and her husband, but can't. A handkerchief in my purse is handy and I take it out to wipe tears rolling down on cheeks. It is unstoppable, like a broken dam. There are still many things in my memory which hurt, but it seems it is our destiny to channel a life path together.

Journal Entry
Toronto, Ontario
October 2, 1995

Lata gives birth to a healthy baby girl on this day. This is the day we celebrate Mahatma Gandhi's birthday. Both mother and baby are doing well. We all are very happy.

A few weeks after my husband's departure for India, I get a call from my daughter Shobha who lives in the US. She suggests that we move there so that she can get help from us with her twins while she plans to finish a teaching credential. So I call my husband and discuss the matter. Finally, I decide to move to the US after two years in Canada and my husband will join me when he comes back.

At the beginning of 1996, I move to the US. My new life in Southern California starts now.

*   *   *

Valencia, California
September 20, 1996

Dear Gojen,

Today I shall write about Jiribam, those days during the 40s. Also, I want to give you a glimpse of how we managed to maintain our culture.

You may be surprised to know how I still remember my childhood days in Jiribam, those days so isolated from the rest of the world. During the 40s there was no transport system from Imphal to Jiribam except walking on foot. There were no proper roads to connect with the rest of the world.

I will write you the story of how my mother and I landed in Jiribam as told by my grandmother later, today's letter is about Jiribam, particularly Babupara where I grew up till the age of 12. I still remember the bungalow we lived in had three bedrooms and a living room. The front verandah/porch was usually used to entertain visitors. There was a phak (mat made out of special grass) spread on sides of the verandah. This mat is still very popular in this part of the country. The bungalows were built in a row facing the East, which was considered good feng shui by Meiteis. On the north side of our bungalow there was a Dak bungalow guest house for visiting officials from Imphal, the state capital of Manipur. To our right, was the same type of bungalow where a Bengali babu (someone who worked as clerical staff in an office) lived. He was a clerk in the same office where my father worked but in a different department. We never saw his family as he never brought them from Cachar district, his home town. He occasionally took leave and visited his family. He always had a helper in the house, though.

I miss those jackfruit trees which father had planted at the sides and plantains and banana trees at the back yard all along the fence. The ripe jackfruits sometimes fell on the ground and we could hear thud sounds at night. In the front yard, we had a blooming champa tree and jasmine flower plants all along the fence. The most unforgettable tree was my grapefruit tree in front of our house outside the gate. It was a signature tree in the whole area of Babupara, maybe in the whole of Jiribam. Even now people who had seen that grape fruit tree still talk about it.

Then in the same row next to our Bengali babu's was a two-storied house made especially to accommodate office attendants like peons, chaprasis and guards. Then a few yards away in the corner was the bungalow of another Bengali babu, who was a head clerk in the civil administrative office. He had his family with small children. Since there was no school in those days, his wife used to teach their kids at home. Next to this corner house was another Bengali babu who worked again in the same department as our next door neighbor. They were known as Amin and were supposed to deal with lands and settlement.

Opposite the head clerk's house across the street was the huge bungalow of the magistrate. As a child I always imagined it to be a king's palace. A big yard all around it was something I presumed could hold at least twenty bungalows like ours. The gate was there without any guard and there were three hundred yards of open space before one could reach the main bungalow.

The hospital was on a hilltop not too far away from our quarters. Along with the hospital there were quarters for the doctors and the compounder pharmacists and other attendants. I don't remember any other doctors' families except Dr. Bharot Singh and Dr. Kirti Singh and Dr. Gopal, some of whose children were of my age and I used to play with them. Lilabati, Sorojini and Basundhari were my playmates until their fathers were transferred. Sorojini, Lilabati's sister, remained close to me for some time during our youth.

Among other families I remember was one in the police department whom my grandmother knew very well as they were far relations from her husband's side. They were a young couple with a very cute daughter. I used to go to their place to help cook, even though I never cooked at home. It was because the lady of the house couldn't enter the cooking area during her monthly period. In our house there was no problem as either my mother or grandmother could do the chore. For the police inspector's family, there was no other help and, hence, I was destined to cook at their kitchen. The police department was on another hillock, which was just opposite to our house, and on the same area stood the civil administration office where my father worked as a clerk.

My favorite pastime was running in the open field chasing our cows to the shede. During the rainy season the stream just before the slope of the hillock where the police and administrative civil office were built. The stream turned into a big lake during monsoon, with lots of small fish swimming around. That was my grandmother's favorite time as she would take out her fishing net and dip it into the new lake. The rainy season was also my happiest of days because the Jiri River swelled up and flooded the village of Kalinagar and the villagers took shelter on our street, which was at a higher level.

The swing my father had made for me under that beautiful umbrella shaped grapefruit tree was my favorite place to spend time. That tree was something nature had crafted with careful precision and its branches spread evenly horizontally. One could climb on it and I used to sit on those branches comfortably. My cousins who came to live in Jiribam during World War II were my playmates and we used to climb on this tree like monkeys. The juicy sweet fruits my grapefruit tree gave were unforgettable gifts.

Every time there was a Hindu festival like Saraswati puja or Durga puja, a special place was made in the corner of our back verandah where a photo of the Goddess of learning was kept and all the books were piled up nearby and prayer was done for three days. On Durga puja time on the fifth day, a type of fish was sacrificed in front of the Goddess Durga and that was the feast of the day. Every time there was some occasion my grandmother made a point to celebrate at home so I never missed any of those Hindu festivals.

Every morning I did my regular prayer in front of the tulsi plant (basil), considered sacred by Hindus burning incense and a lamp near it. Those days incense was a crystal-like substance and when it was burnt it gave out fumes and smell to purify the air outside and inside the house. There was a reserved area known as Sanamahi at the corner of the South West side of the house. The incense was also burnt in the front verandah as a daily ritual of prayer twice daily onc time in the morning and another in the evening. It was daily routine.

The locality known as Babupara housed government employees clustered in this area and surrounded by villages those villages—Dibong, Lamba Sarak and Kalinagar. These villages were inhabited by Meities. The hill areas were inhabited by different tribes. Not too far away from our quarter were three shops owned by Bengali families. We had a weekly market on Fridays at our side while the Monday market was at the other side of the Jiri River. The tea garden at the other side of the Jiri River belonged to the Cachar district. There was an elementary school for the tea garden children. Once father put me there but when he found out that the standard of the school was just to make the children learn how to sign their names, he immediately took me out. Those were the days the British still ruled India and Indians were fighting for independence. But in Jiribam we hardly knew about the revolution going on in the rest of India. This much for today. With lots of love.

Yours lovingly,
Ine

*   *   *

Journal Entry
Valencia, California
March 20, 1996

Once I settle in Valencia near Los Angeles with my daughter Shobha and her family, finishing beauty college become my priority as I want to pursue a career as a cosmetologist.

Shobha takes me to join the college and I am glad that I can complete the course earlier than usual as I have hours from previous classes in New Delhi and also from Southampton Community College in Toronto.

Journal Entries
Valencia, California
February 16, 1997

Today the the 16th of February turns out to be worst thunderstorm affecting the course of my life. The unexpected call from a family friend, Mr. Hazarika, who was our neighbor in Shillong comes as a whirlpool and I am inside this. I have been waiting for a call from Rup as he is in Shillong at this time. Instead, Mr. Hazarika is on the line. It is a frantic call. "Mr. Advani is in Nazareth Hospital and is in the intensive care unit." Then there is a pause.

The shocking news strikes me into helpless situation and I am stunned. I can't talk further but manage to ask, "Is he conscious?"

"No, he is in coma, and Tuleswer is with him." Tuleswer, my brother, has been accompanying him during his journey to Shillong from Delhi. My daughter who is standing by my side takes the phone from me and she continues to talk to Mr. Hazarika for few minutes.

She puts the phone back. "Mom, you should get ready immediately for India. Mr. Hazarika is at present having guests for his son's wedding. He couldn't talk longer." I am completely numbed by this sudden sad news and everything is shattered into pieces. My husband has been planning to come to California in April. Will that plan remain to be fulfilled?

Now for my leaving the country I need to have permission from the US government since my papers for a green card are in process. But the next day is President's Day and offices are closed. I now have to wait till the offices are open the next day.

February 17, 1997

The second phone call comes and it is the most dreaded one. "Rup passed away at 11:20 AM on 17th February 1997."

He has left us all forever without saying goodbye to me and to our children.

Gone

His and mine
Brick by brick
Layer by layer
Fountain of hopes
Many seasons
And the mansion
Stood elegantly
His and mine
The dream house!
One stormy night

Fierce wind
And thunder
A lightening strike
Trapped inside
To hold his hands
He was not there
I cried
I knew then

"Mom, you could reach there in time for the cremation. We should book the air ticket immediately." In India, we usually do the cremation immediately. Shobha has just informed both Lata, my oldest daughter, and Jibesh, my son in Toronto, Canada.

I apply for permission to leave the country the day after President's Day. As I couldn't reach in time for my husband's funeral, my son leaves for New Delhi and then to Shillong where Rup's body is kept at our relative and friend, Mr. Tuku Dutt's house in Laban (unlike Meitei custom.)

For the last one and half years we had talked on the phone, but not seen each other. Now Rup can't even talk to me. My wait for his arrival at California is nipped in the bud. The reality of my future as widow is in front of me. I feel all alone in this whole universe.

Figure 2 Jamuna and Rup in 1970s

I take the flight to Delhi as soon as I receive permission to leave the country. My sister-in-law Meera joins me on the journey to her brother-in-law's house in Shillong. We reach Guwahati, take a taxi to Shillong, another three and half hours drive in addition to the two-hour flight. On the day of the funeral, Mr. Tuku Dutt, Meera's brother-in-law, has arranged everything, including the procession to the cremation ground. The local Sindhi community also has prepared the ritual to be performed according to Hindu rites. The most amazing thing is my husband's lifeless body has been lying in their house for more than 24 hours waiting for my son, Jibesh to come and do the ritual a son has to perform. I shall never be able to pay back the services the Dutt family has done. I am indebted to them forever. When I meet people around in this small town, they express their love and concern for Rup; they have done what they could do for him. Rup had been living in and out of this area for years. So everyone seemed to know him very well, even before we built the house in Shillong. Today his soul remains in this crematorium with a silent gratitude toward all who had come to say farewell to him. We reach Shillong one day after the funeral. We arrange for the final ritual to be performed by the priest after five days. I leave for Imphal, Jibesh for Canada via Kalikota and Meera for Delhi.

I reach Imphal, and I find the condition of my mother beyond my imagination. She is bed-ridden and weakened with old age. She is constantly having diarrhea at the same time for which treatment is being given by doctor. She looks at me and I feel she wants to talk but cannot communicate with me as before. I just sit near to talk to her. She understands me.

My Mother's Last Days

My mother lies on her bed
Weak with old age
Long lustrous black hair
Now in a silver grey braid

Her face so gentle, and calm.
Three springs passed
When I am back to see her.
Mom, I call. She opens her eyes.
I see a glimpse of happiness
then drops of tear on her cheeks.
She knows about Rup, my husband,
Whose funeral service was a week ago.
I feel the pain in my heart
To see her so weak and helpless.
I sit next to her holding her hand
Silent, two hearts murmuring to each other.
Eight days pass, slight improvement,
the ninth day my brother informs me
Maiba, priest for the final journey of life,
Has been called;
I rush toward her bed,
See her eyes
Closed
Hear her heavy breath.
Mom, do not go so soon.
I sit close to her, her head on my lap,
My hand stroking her hair
She seems so much at peace.
And she has gone home to Eternity
This day the 4th of March, 1997.
Both my dearest, closest ones
Have left me forever.
I return to America with silent tears.

I leave Imphal for Kolkata where I have to meet life insurance agents. Rup used to handle this himself. All decisions have to be made by me now, alone, as I have no one to consult. The funniest part of our life is that Rup always believed in astrology and palmistry. One who wrote horoscopes for my children once predicted that I would never become widow. I would die before my husband. Rup took it quite seriously and hence took out a good amount of life insurance is in my name. Now I have to pay for all this till the maturity date. Even the beneficiary of Rup's insurance is not me but our son, as he was so convinced that I would be the one to leave this universe first. But nothing is certain about life.

*   *   *

Valencia, California
August 10, 1997

Dear Gojen

My letters to you are partly to show you and future generations something about the life we used to have. One day I will join the ancestors of future generations. That is why I want to leave behind the legacy of our family along with knowledge of the social behavior of my time. I do hope we keep in touch as promised earlier. Today's writing is about another incident in Jiribam. It was Monday morning, spring of 1945 as I watched Father getting ready for the office. I wanted to ask for a new notebook. Mother was in the kitchen early to make lunch before 9:30 am so that he could have lunch and leave for his office. For children, left over rice with curry was usually kept aside and this left over food children ate in between meals; it was known as charawanba.

I still remember that big kitchen hall and the cooking area at the far end corner on the right hand side and always kept separately not to be entered by anyone other than the assigned person to cook. Only who cooked food could enter the place Known as Chak Khum. In the middle of the hall was an area for dining. Away from this area, on the other side, was a permanent fireplace known as Phunga, where fire was kept alive with logs of wood and compacted husks from rice. This place was used for boiling water or making tea. We used to sit around feeding logs of woods to the fire while waiting for dinner to be ready. That was the time we spent chitchatting particularly during winter months.

Figure 3 Crossing Jiri river by boat

That morning Father finished his bath in the backyard near the well and changed into muga Khudai (a robe smaller than a Dhoti, made out of muga, a type of silk thread). Once he came inside and sat on the mat where the special place was kept bordered with sticks on three sides, he took out the chandan from the Laiphu (a small box containing idols and images for worshipping). He took out three shining stones and the picture of Lord Krishna and nicely arranged after chandan tikka was put on his forehead. Chandan tikka was just like the white tikka on the forehead put on by Hare Krishna devotees. That was usually applied after bath and before meals by the folks in Manipur who are Hindu Meities. Father ate his lunch after his ritual of worship, as usual grumbling about the food. We ate and found it quite good. If Father liked the food, he ate quietly without saying anything as appreciation. But that was his way. Mother was used to it. I watched Father finish his early meal and go out on the verandah to wash his hands with water from the special mug made of brass known as Khujai. Then he went to the bedroom and changed from his Khudai into trousers and a shirt, which was kept ready for his office. I waited till the last minute to ask for the notebook, which I needed for school. I was always nervous to ask him for anything. I said, "Pabung, I need to buy a notebook for my home work."

Father looked at me with a little smile, "I had been wondering why you looked so anxious to say something." I could sense he was in a good mood.

He continued, "We'll buy it today; it will be cheaper if we get it from the Monday market after I come back from office." Then he left.

The civil office where my father worked as a clerk was about a 1/4 mile away from our quarter. He was the only Meitei Manipuri among the staff of the civil office. Since all his office staffs were Bengalis, father picked up the Bengali dialect very well. Since the Bengali script was the same as our script, meiteilol/manipuri, he always read Bengali literature and drama. When father said that he would be taking me to the market, I was so thrilled with excitement. That day after I finished my meal, took out my school bag and walked out of the front gate for school, I hardly had gone ten steps from the front gate, when my grandmother called me back. I wondered why and turned back toward her. She stood there with a comb and held my chin towards her, "Is this the way to comb your hair?"

I thought the style a good one, my hair combed straight down. I had my hair boy-cut style and it was growing out now.

"You need to part straight and comb sideways." She fixed my hair according to her way. I didn't fuss over it. She would have done the way she liked any way. When she was satisfied, she let me go. I walked skip jumping in between rocks, most of the time with a happy tune inside my head. The path was mostly grass and stones, sometime muddy. But there were green grass

all around. I was more excited about my going to the market and did practice my tables for the math home work on the way. Our school was over by three pm and I came back home almost running. After I ate rice and curry, which was kept for me to eat after school, I waited for my father. He normally came back home by five but that day he was late and I was worried in case we did not have time enough for shopping. There was no sign of father at 5:20 and I was more worried. It was 5:30 when I saw him coming toward our house. I was so relieved.

I waited anxiously while he took water from the bucket with a mug and washed his face and then feet. He wiped with the cotton khudei (towel) which was woven on the family loom by Mother and Grandmother. He sat down on his favorite chair waiting for his tea. This was his routine. He called. "Ibemhal, where is my tea? Hurry up. I have to take Jamuna to market."

My mother just then entered the room with a cup of tea and some biscuits. Father loved his tea. Every two or three hours he used to ask mother for tea, especially on holidays. After he finished his tea and had some biscuits, he looked relaxed. Getting up from the chair, he called "Jamuna, are you ready? Let's go." He started walking out of the door.

"I'm ready," I let him know and followed him. We walked for about fifteen minutes to the bank of the Jiri River. To go to the Monday market we had to take the boat to cross the Jiri River. We reached the spot and saw the boat already left the shore and it was almost in midstream. We had to wait for its return to our side of the bank. Monday market was always on the other side of the river at Jirighat where the tea garden was situated. When he saw the boat coming back he gave me one rupee and told me, "Take this money for your notebook and ferry fare."

"Aren't you coming?" I asked, surprised. I was hoping he would come with me. At nine years old, I had never gone alone to the market

"No I am staying here; I'll wait for you at this spot. Go and get your notebook fast." Even though I was still disappointed, I couldn't do anything about it.

"Oh, the boat is almost here. I have to go fast." I responded. I ran down the bank toward the boat, which had just anchored so that the passengers could board. We waited for everyone to get out and then slowly we all got in one by one. When my turn came I handed over one rupee note to the boatman for fare, and waited for change from the boatman.

"Baby, here is your change." I took the change and counted exact ninety paise. When the boat reached the other side of the river, I got off and I ran up the steep bank of the river and then toward the market. I saw the crowd of the market and walked hurriedly toward it. The shops were all temporary stalls. I looked around to find the stalls where the stationery supplies were sold. I had gone with my grandmother to the market before and hence I knew a little bit of the area. As I passed through the rows of fish vendors, the stench and fishy smell hit my nose. The raw fishy smell was too much; I closed my nose with my left fingers. I walked faster to get away from the smell. After crossing a few rows of vegetable vendors I found the place where stalls for stationery supplies were set up. I went to the second shop as it looked to have more items than the others. I selected one notebook, gave the shopkeeper the thirty paise, the amount he asked for. I grabbed the notebook with my right hand and returned the same way I had come. When I reached the bank where the boat was anchored, the boatman was waiting a few minutes more for passengers to come. I took out ten paise and paid him for return fare.

When the boat reached the bank where my father waited, I impatiently got out of the boat and ran toward him. He was there sitting on the rock looking toward the river and looked relieved to see me with the notebook, happy that I had come back *safe after doing the shopping all alone. Panting and breathless from running up on the slope of the bank, I handed over the fifty paise change. "Pabung, here is the change.' I stood there proudly thinking that I had accomplished a great job by myself. He took the change and counted it. I saw in his face, the sudden change of his mood and I could tell something was wrong. He said that the shopkeeper charged me too much.*

"I don't care if we have to spend more for the ferry fare; you have to learn the right way. The shopkeeper had no right to cheat a child. Go and get back ten paise, otherwise return it and buy from another." I had no choice. With a sullen face looking down on the ground I went back to the boat.

I again paid the fare to the boatman while he looked at me in surprise wondering why I had to go back to the market.

"Baby, you are back again?" the boatman asked me. I just gave a wry smile and handed him his fare and sat quietly. I was not sure if I could find the location of the stall. It was getting late and some of the shops must have left by then. I was worried and terribly confused. Once I was out of the boat taking the same route, the fishy stinky smell didn't bother me. My concern for finding the shop was more important than anything else. It was even more confusing to look for the same spot among the many rows of the temporary stalls as some of the stalls were now empty and the shop keepers had left the place. I stood there at the corner looking around and couldn't figure out the location of the shop. As more shops one by one started packing up to leave, I became panicky. I went around the stalls again but I couldn't find the one I had gotten my notebook from. The sky seemed to be turning greyer and it would be dark shortly. I stood battling myself whether to go back now or continue to look for it. I finally turned toward the direction of the boat. I knew what father's reaction would be, but I couldn't do anything else either. I arrived at the same spot where he sat waiting for me.

"Pabung, I could not find the shop, couldn't get the money back." I handed the remaining money left after paying the ferry fare. I could hardly hear my own pathetic voice.

He didn't say a word. I could see the anger and disappointment in his eyes. He stood up and without a word, started walking briskly toward home. I followed him almost running to keep pace with him with the notebook under my arm. Though it was evening, and the sun had already set, it was still very hot in Jiribam. Sweat trickled into my notebook and so I switched it into my left hand. At the same time I was worried and scared because I knew there would be more haranguing and a barrage once we reached home.

I still wonder why Father let me go back again wasting money for the ferry fare. When I ponder over it now, I have come to the conclusion that he wanted me to be bold and have self confidence. Only I wish he could have shown me in a softer tone. But it was his way. I shall be writing you more again.

Yours lovingly,
Ine

*   *   *

Journal Entry
Valencia, California
October 10, 1997

After about six months in Beauty College, with hours from my previous training, I can take the test and get my license as a cosmetologist. There is a job waiting for me at Fantastic Sam's, owned by an Indian lady from Kalikota, Ms. Lena Patel. Also I am getting my first car in the US from my daughter as she transfers her Nissan Sentara in my name. I love Valencia, a suburban area with a mixed community. I have come across quite a few ladies who are now my good friends. Gina, who is in the same profession, talks about Reiki, a healing touch from a Japanese technique introduced by Mikau Usui. It is believed that it was a healing art practiced by the Tibetan monks in ancient times. Gina learned in Mumbai that it has become very popular there. I am quite curious and when I come across an advertisement about it, I immediately contact Ms Gail Verbos who is a Reiki Master/Teacher. I don't think twice before joining Gail Verbos' classes at Angel's Corner, 23300 Cinema Drive Valencia, CA. I am so fascinated by it that I complete up to the master level and then later the teacher's level. Angel's Corner becomes a place for our group to meet regularly for spiritual discussions and meditations. Here I meet Myrna who has become one of my best friends and we plan for many cruises together.

Journal Entry
San Ramon, California
December 1999

Now a big change takes place, as my son-in-law Lall plans to move to Northern California for his job in the technical field. We move to San Ramon, a suburban town about 45 minutes drive from the city of San Francisco. Now we have to get acquainted with new streets and shops. Also we need to get to know people. I go to the Senior Center for volunteer work. I have been given the task of helping in the kitchen.

This time has given me a complete change in my perspective of life. Even though I feel so lonely sometimes and down emotionally, life moves on. Time is a healer. Gradually I decide to do the things I have been longing to do while I am still well and alive. The universe is so beautiful and I want to enjoy it.

Valencia, California
November 3, 1997

Dear Gojen

Here again about an incident. I still remember this day during my childhood in Jiribam. It was the day when I watched with interest while my father made me a kite. Sitting down on the floor of the back verandah, I was happy that Sunday morning watching my father transform those papers and bamboo sticks into a colorful kite with its tail. It was my father's first project of the day as he hadn't resumed his carpentry hobby. Most Sundays he used to make wooden furniture for the family with skillful artistry. We still have those decorative wooden beds and cupboards in our ancestral home.

He took out his favorite knife and a pair of scissors and on the floor, laid down those colored papers, which he had purchased from the local shop the previous day. I watched every step in the process of his making that kite. One bamboo stick was trimmed thin enough to bend into the shape of a bow when string was tied at both ends and then an arrow shaped thin stick was attached crosswise. Then the bamboo structure was attached to a 14"x14" square paper with glue made out of from boiled rice. Finally, this was laid in the sun to dry while he made a long strip of the remaining paper for the kite's tail.

He then attached the tail to the kite at the end of the arrow; Father again left it to dry completely in the sun. It didn't take long to dry. After it was dried completely, he tied the thread from the roll of thread to it. After about 15 minutes, it was ready. He looked satisfied with the finished kite and asked, "Are you ready to run with the kite?" I was thrilled and nodded yes.

He led me with the kite toward the open field in front of our quarter. I followed him with excitement. My grandmother as usual was busy at the back verandah weaving on the loom and I informed her about our plan.

"Grandma, I am going to the field. Trying my kite."

"Come back in time for lunch," was her response.

"All right, I'll be back." It was about 9.30 am and hence I had time to play for more than an hour before the lunch. As it was Sunday we would have our meals a bit later than usual. Father helped me get the kite up into the air and then he went back inside our house, leaving me to play alone. With the April wind blowing slowly to welcome me, I ventured toward all directions of the field. I ran from one end of the field to the other holding the string. When I saw my kite soaring high up in the sky, I was still so thrilled with excitement, the string wrapped dowel in my right hand. The blue sky with scattered clouds drew wind, giving my kite the strength to soar higher and higher as I pulled the string to and fro. The kite seemed exhilarated, rising further and further up, and the clouds looked amused at my experimental trial. What a lovely time I had in my own world having fun with my kite. Then I saw those two teenage boys approach toward my direction.

I recognized them as the sons of a constable from the Police Department. I saw them standing and watching me play, still running with my kite. They seemed to be interested in my kite, and I even thought to myself if they wanted to play with *it I shall let them for a while. I continued running around as before. But suddenly I realized the kite was shifting its direction to the opposite side as one of the boys ran toward their quarter which was on top of the hillock opposite ours. The suddenness of his pulling away the dowel from my hand gave me a surprise and I was stunned. The younger boy followed him running, looking back again and again with his teeth showing.*

I shouted, "Give me back, give me back my kite," and ran after them. My kite was still in the air fluttering, no longer flying high up.

"What're you doing? It's my kite. Give it back," I shouted at the top of my lungs. As they disappeared behind the Civil Office, I stopped running still ranting and panting. I watched the direction where they were no longer within my view. They were no match for me as they ran much faster. I stood helpless, tears welling up in my eyes; even though I tried to control myself, I sobbed. I wished I could cry out loudly to make them hear me, but I couldn't. Slowly I turned back and walked toward home, my tears still streaming down my cheeks. As soon as I entered our home, I saw my grandmother sitting in the verandah, and I ran straight to her, put my arms around her, my face buried in her cotton shawl. She saw I had come back without my kite.

"What happened? Why you are crying?" she asked. I could not control myself and could mutter only a few words at a time.

"Those two boys from the police quarters came and snatched my kite." She looked at me in disbelief. Father was busy working on his carpentry and didn't hear me. Surprisingly, grandmother got up and told him. He looked surprised and disappointed. But instead of consoling me, what he said to me was something I could never forget.

"You should have run after them till you got your kite back."

My grandmother was quite upset. "Those boys are big boys. How could she run after them?" She looked at me and said, "There will be another kite. Don't worry. I am going to talk to their parents."

I felt good hearing my grandmother and my sobbing slowly lessened. My mother brought a wet khudei (towel) and wiped my face. Then she went to the kitchen to serve lunch for us. I sat down on the small mat and pulled my pukham (brass plate containing cooked rice and dal in tenkot (small bowls) toward me. On the side of the plate were stir fried vegetables and fish fry. As I didn't like vegetables my mother did not give me much. It was around 11 am. We usually had lunch around this time on Sundays. Father was at the opposite side while my grandmother sat at the right-hand side with me sitting next to her. My mother was busy serving everyone and she usually had her food after everyone was served. As usual she tried to finish my father's leftovers. A wife could take her husband's leftovers, but never vice versa. The husband was supposed to be considered as God for the woman.

I did get another kite the following weekend. Grandmother managed to talk to the boys' parents. They never came back to trouble me after that day's incident. Those kite snatchers, I wonder sometimes what became of them. As a police constable, their father might have been transferred to Imphal or some other district since their terms in one place were only for two years. My father's remark, made from his frustration at the time, instilled in me a feeling of timidity, rather than the confidence he wanted me to have. I wish I could change him.

The year 1942 was a tragic year for Japanese Americans as they were kept locked up so that they couldn't oppose the war effort. Their internment all over the West Coast was ordered by Congress and FDR had to execute the law. A more optimistic

landmark came in January of that year when the first black student was admitted to the University of Tennessee, US A.
  This is all for today.

Yours lovingly,
Ine

*   *   *

Journal Entry
Las Vegas
October 7, 1998

Finally my son Jibesh decides to marry Colleen, a Canadian girl. He has had dates with a couple of girls after coming back from Ireland and now he has found the love of his life. Both are in love they say and hence they decide on a wedding to be performed in Las Vegas. We all go to Las Vegas for the wedding tomorrow. The bride and groom as usual look very elegant. I am so happy to see my son getting married. Rup would have been so happy to see his son settled.

Almost all our relatives have come. His bride Colleen is accompanied by her mother and sister and her stepfather. After the wedding, Shobha and Lall will give a reception party for all the guests. Then everyone will disperse and do their own activities.

Journal Entries
San Ramon, California
January 14, 2000

We celebrate my son-in-law Lall's birthday at his sister Priya's house in San Jose. Meeting Priya's in-laws and their relatives turns out to be a bit of a formal affair. Today someone gives me advice about how one can get disability benefits from Social Security. But I am not in favor of this. I work for my benefits and when the time comes, I shall get my share according to my contribution. I wonder why one should try to give unwanted advice; it is a waste of energy and creates unnecessary misunderstanding. This is a good lesson for me, too.

January 16, 2000

We give a housewarming party in San Ramón. Many friends and relatives come to attend the party. Since I still help by taking my grand kids to school and picking them up, I am lucky that I can still work part-time. I am thankful to God for my health and that I have such caring people around.

February 17, 2000,

Today is the third anniversary of Rup's death. Another three years have passed so quickly. The Sradha ritual, an offering to God and the dear ones, is performed at the Livermore Hindu temple complex at one of the quarters of the priests. It is not usually done at the temple when we are invoking the death and doing prayer for their souls to rest in peace. According to the Hindus, a son usually performs the ritual on particular days of October and November by offering food and flowers to the God and the souls of the departed ones.

February 19, 2000

I join JC Penney's Beauty Salon. This is my first job offer here and I am happy. Even though I receive another job offer from another salon, I join JC Penney. I sort of like the atmosphere. Inside the Mall it is a good place to walk around and do window shopping during lunch hour. I love watching people go about their mundane activities.

February 22, 2000

I got a traffic ticket for the first time for turning right without stopping. This is a lesson for me as I have had the habit of laughing at people caught by traffic police, amused by their situation. This is a lesson I learn today.

March 4, 2000

Today is the 3rd anniversary of my mother's death. How time slips away. I wonder sometimes if she is with my father. I always feel her absence whenever I visit my brother's home in Imphal. As long as one's mother is alive, the feeling of being a child remains always inside one's heart. When a mother has gone away, that feeling is shattered.

I meet Ms Marie Boss who is a Buddhist and she talks about chanting. I am curious and want to experience the Buddhist practice of Nichiren Daisonin, and hence join the group. I meet mostly whites and a few South Americans but no Indians and no African Americans. May 4, 2001 Marie and her friend Jeannie take me to Soka Gokkai International East Bay meeting in San Francisco. I get some books from there. Now I am getting involved with Soka Gokkai International, USA.

The Bay Area is a place we enjoy both the beauty of the snow clad mountains as well as the open beaches where one is captivated with the vast ocean and its waves dancing to and fro. Our city of San Ramon has newly developed housing areas as well old ones. One can choose either and enjoy. Bent Creek housing is the area where we live, and it is just at the border of city of Dublin. The city of Danville is also next to our city to the northeast. We see large open land across the way toward Danville where cows and horses graze.

The house Lall and Shobha have here at Bent Creek housing is only five years old. They are the second owners. The upper floor has three bedrooms including the master bedroom. Out of the two bathrooms, one common bathroom is shared by their three sons. One room was shared by twin sons Lucas and Leon and the room on northwest side is occupied by their oldest son Dev. The study area is open and used as office with computers and a printer. Downstairs one guest room and a bathroom are given to me. The living room just at the entrance has a cream color leather sofa set with cupboard near the wall where all their books and displays are arranged nicely. One step down is the formal dining area and then the closet, bathroom and the guest room I occupy. Opposite the closet space, leading to the kitchen is the family sitting area used most of the time, a common place for all of us.

The small space for informal dining is used to the maximum. The view of the backyard from the window is exquisite and everyone who comes compliments on our backyard. The colored shrubs all around, the roses in their reserved space and the tall pine trees on both sides near the fencing provide a grand view of this exceptionally beautiful landscape.

I join Las Positas Community College for computer classes and also medical transcription classes at the Hayward adult school. Finally, I realize that to work as a transcriptionist there is too much strain on my hand and fingers. I drop the idea of becoming one.

* * *

Valencia, California
July 25, 1998

Dear Gojen,

I was surprised myself when grandmother narrated her life story about how we happened to be in Jiribam. It was such an unexpected turn of life; I found it fascinating. I think you may feel the same way.

My grandmother Sanachaubi was the one who initiated bringing mom and me to Jiribam. Today's letter is all about our journey so you and future generations of our family will have some idea about our traditions and the culture of that era.

The summer of 1942 in Jiribam, the temperature was high and we were experiencing the melting point by the afternoon. We sat under a hand-pulled ceiling fan in our living room, which my mother or grandmother pulled, trying to feel cool air from its gentle blow. Father had gone to work, hence only three of us were at home.

We all had wet khudei (towels) nearby so that we could use them as a cooling device, wiping our faces occasionally. We felt like we were almost sitting on a furnace.

"I wish we were in Imphal. We never used a fan there where the weather is always pleasant," my grandmother sort of grumbled.

"Why are we here, and not in Imphal?" I asked, giving her a questioning look.

"Come here." Brushing the stool next to her with her hand, Grandma signaled me to sit down next to her. I took the seat and waited for her story to start. When she unfolded the history of her life as well as ours, my curiosity grew intense.

It is a long story," she said. "I got married to your grandfather as arranged by my parents at the age of 13. His (yumnak{last name) was Khetrimayum, which was considered as one of the high ranks in the caste system and that was the reason he was chosen by my parents. My husband and I lived with his parents at a locality called Sagolband in the same town Imphal.

Your grandfather was the only son and as his older sister was already married, we lived in the same house along with my in-laws. As arranged by our parents, neither of us met before the wedding took place.

"The day after our wedding I was busy doing whatever I had to do as a new bride getting up early in the morning before anyone else was awake. I finished mopping the front verandah and got ready for the elders' ritual for prayer. Some jasmine flowers that I plucked from the yard were placed on the copper plate and clean fresh water from the pond was collected in a brass jar. I placed all near the Tulsi plant in the front yard.

"Later, I had a Hidakphu (hookah) ready for my father-in-law. Hidakphu is a pot and a pipe connected to it while

the tobacco mixture is burnt inside a small cylindrical container on top of the pot and puffed through the pipe. My father-in-law usually smoked after his morning ritual. That was the accepted custom and norm for the elders once they were married and had children."

Figure 4 Hookah/Hidakphu

Then Grandma kept herself quiet for some time. In a subdued tone with a slightly controlled giggle, she said, "After completing all the work for the house before my in-laws awoke, I was ready to go inside to the kitchen to prepare for lunch. I saw a young man entering the front gate. I wondered why he had come to our house so early in the morning. I rolled out a mat at the front verandah for him to sit down on as it was customary, showing courtesy to a guest. But he didn't say a word to acknowledge it and quietly entered the front door. I was puzzled and wondered why he did so."

I saw my grandmother's face broke into wide smile and said, "Can you believe it? He was my husband, your grandfather and I didn't recognize him."

I was amused and couldn't believe what I just heard, "You didn't recognize your own husband?" As the marriage was arranged by both the parents the bride and the groom were not given a chance to see each other before the wedding. After she told me this incident, she smiled a bit and was quiet again, reminiscing about the precious moments of her youth when she was young and innocent.

Then she continued to tell about her life. Her daughter, Ibemhal, was the first child after three years of their marriage. Then a second daughter, Ibeyaima, was born within one and half years. Third daughter, Ibetombi, was born after two more years. When Ibemhal was eight years old, your grandfather became very sick with tuberculosis."

My grandmother could not escape what destiny had brought to her life. There was no cure for tuberculosis during those days and my maternal grandfather had succumbed to this terrible ailment making her a widow with three little girls. She was helpless as her in-laws also were no longer alive. To get support after the loss of her husband, she had to make the choice of moving to her brother's home, which was their ancestral home in Ningthem Macha Kollup at Yumnam Leikai, Yaiskul. I learned that the families on my grandmother's side had lots of farm land/ paddy fields in the villages and when rice season came, they used to get their share from the villagers bags of paddies.

My grandmother's suffering didn't end there. Her little daughter, the youngest one, became very sick with high fever and never recovered from it. While staying with her brother's family, she earned her living partly by weaving in the loom. She wove different types of cloths such as Phanek (dresses for the local women), Kokyet (turban), and Innaphi (a broad scarf for women) and Dhoti (worn by men).

I again started asking her about our arrival at Jiribam. She said, "I am coming to that."

She started to narrate her story, and I listened to her intensely, spellbound. My mother was only fifteen when the proposal for marriage came from my father's side. They found it to be a good proposal since Father worked for the government. His previous wife just left him with their daughter and never came back. So father agreed to his mother's choice of the girl and hence both sides of the family decided to have a simple ceremony as my grandmother was not in a financial position to provide a proper wedding. Father took leave for a few days and came to Imphal to get married. After one week of the simple ceremony,

Father left for Jiribam. My mother stayed back at Keishampat in her in-law's house with my paternal grandmother, Leinau, a widow, and my Aunt Pashot, who was a single mother with a son and one more on the way. My mother took care of household affairs like cooking for the family, washing, and cleaning while her in-laws were engaged in their business.

After a few weeks my mother Ibemhal found out that she was pregnant with me. I was born on March 21st 1935 at Keishampat, Imphal. This year is significant one as United States' Social Security Act was passed in August. Also this is the year in June that Smith and Wilson formed Alcoholics Anonymous. Another important event was In November when the University of Maryland admitted a black student, Donald Murray.

My mother still waited impatiently for my father because even after I was born, he never tried to come back to Imphal for his wife and newborn daughter.

An unprecedented circumstance changed our destiny. One day my grandmother Sanachaubi was on her way to the market and had to pass Keishampat on the way. She had with her handloom products to sell in the Khwaramband Bazaar at Ima Keithel (Mother's Market). She decided to stop by and see her daughter and grandchild. She explained to me that the day's product was Kokyet (turban), which was used to

Figure 5 aunt Pahot Devi

wrap around the heads of men in the Sikh communities. Sikh traders in Imphal used to buy from the local market for their use and also for trading. They were business people who came from

Punjab in search of better opportunities. Kokyets were woven at the handloom and sold at the market by Meitei womenfolk.

Something made her mind say to go and see my mother and me, and thus that day, our destiny was marked as she entered the gate of her daughter's house. She withdrew deep into her thoughts again before she started to tell me the rest of the story.

I touched her shoulder slightly and asked her, "What's happened?" She gave me a startled look as if I had awakened her from sleep.

Sorry, my mind drifted away. That day after my lunch around 11 in the morning, I started from home at Yumnam Leikai, took the short cut through the swinging bridge of Numbul Turel and came via Elangbam Leikai, then Keishamthong and reached Keishampat. When I reached the Keishampat junction, I couldn't resist turning toward you father's house. I passed through Lai Sumang of Keishampat Leirambi and then the path by the side of bamboo bushes, then the entrance leading to the gate."

She took a deep breath and continued her story.

"I tried to pull the bamboo poles through the holes of the two posts of the gate so that I could walk toward the house. I heard a loud cry of a baby from somewhere, and I realized the cry was from the verandah of the house I was going to. I could see the baby lying there on the mat and crying. Also I saw your grandmother Leinou and your aunt Pashot at the other end of the verandah absorbed in their work. I was surprised as none of them picked up the baby."

She said my aunt Pashot was busy making potloi (costume dress for the Rasleela dance), also used as bridal dress. She was so absorbed in her work, she didn't raise her head when grandmother approached the verandah. Aunt Pashot was expert in making those dresses and her products were very much in demand. Along with it she made those colorful dresses for Lord

Krishna in the Rasleela performance, a part of the religious offering to the Lord.

Leinou, at the same time, was busy making artificial jewelry (imitation of gold jewelry). Only when my grandmother picked up the baby and held the baby in her arms did both of them look up.

They asked my grandmother how long ago she had arrived there. They didn't even notice someone coming to their house. That was how much they were involved in their business. Grandmother said she tried to calm down the baby and with the corner of the broad scarf she was wearing, wiped the tears of the baby. She was sure that the baby was very hungry.

Grandmother decided to go inside the house to feed the baby as my mother Ibemhal was nowhere to be seen. Her in-laws resumed their work. Once she was inside she could get the aroma of the fried onion and maroi, a locally grown herb. My mother gave a look of surprise more so when she saw the baby in my grandmother's arm. Those tears still trickling down the baby's cheeks, Grandmother continued wiping them with the corner of her scarf. She now realized why my mother was not able to come out to feed the baby. She was cooking lunch for the family so that she could serve lunch to everyone in time. Those days till the sixties, in our community, a woman who did cooking had to have a shower and change her clothes into a washed phanek (skirt) or one made out of muga (silk) material before she entered the kitchen. When she was in the kitchen cooking, she couldn't touch anyone else outside. Mother couldn't leave the cooking halfway.

Another thing was that a woman of Meitei during her monthly period could not cook for the family for five days until her isolation was over. She could resume her normal household duties only after she had completely bathed including washing her hair with a specially prepared lotion known as Chenghi on the fifth day. For Chenghi, the water from washing the uncooked rice is boiled with leaves of various citrus fruits like lemon and other leaves of aromatic plants. Then after cooling it down, it was to be used for washing hair. Most of the women had very thick, lustrous, long dark black hair.

Grandmother filled the bottle with milk and after feeding the baby she felt something was not right. After she saw mother was able to take care of the baby she left for the market to sell her handloom products at Mother's Market, still a unique, well-known tourist spot in Imphal as it is run by women only.

Grandmother Sanachaubi walked toward the market thinking about the incident. It was like a storm slowly sweeping through the sky; she couldn't stop thinking about it. Even after a few days, this nagging memory continued and my grandmother felt she had to do something. She finally came up with a plan. She decided whatever happened, she would take her daughter and the baby to Jiribam, where her son-in-law, Ibungohal Singh worked.

Once she made up her mind, she had to make a plan of action even though she knew it was a difficult task. She immediately started to find out from different sources how to go to Jiribam. There were two different ways, one way was to go by bus via Kohima town to Dimaprur, a foothill town of Nagaland, and then take a train from there to Silchar, a town in Cachar district near Jiribam. It would take three days. But she needed someone who knew the common Indian language Hindusthani to go with her during the journey. Neither Grandmother nor my mother knew any other language except our own dialect Meiteilol. Since it was to cost her a lot more far beyond her means, Grandmother decided to take the alternate route.

They had to walk for several days on the hilly terrain of Imphal-Cachar road known as Tongjei Maril. It was difficult, especially for women who had not walked up the hill before.

Imphal's valley people could not imagine how one traveled on the hills. (Nowadays the road is made for buses and trucks).

Grandmother managed to hire two local men as porters, one for the baby to be carried on his back and the other porter to carry the luggage. She then found out that some traders also were planning to travel via that road within a few days. After she completed all the arrangements, she informed my mother's in-laws about their plan to leave Imphal for Jiribam. My paternal grandmother was surprised, but happy to hear about her plan. So after getting permission from my paternal grandmother Leinou to take my mother and me to Jiribam, my grandmother was ready to start her journey along with those traders on an auspicious day as told by the astrologers/priest in autumn of 1935.

Since I was born in March 1935, by the time I traveled, I must have been about eight months old. When those leaves turned orange and the sky was blue, on that particular auspicious day my grandmother, my mother, and I, along with the two porters, joined the group of traders and travelers for the long journey to Jiribam on Tongjei Maril (Tongjei Maril means twisted long pipe of the hookah), the name given to Imphal—Cachar Road. The porter carried me on his back with the support of a long cloth tied across his chest (it is a very popular method in our area for carrying and inducing babies to sleep) known as poba. Those traders regularly frequented that road to trade with the hill tribes and people living in Cachar and other parts of Assam. I believe those days people were not used to any footwear. If it there was any, it was meant for the affluent and royal families. Those were made of fabrics. Common people sometimes had footwear made up of a wooden platform known as khurum with an attachment in between the big toe and next toe. Shoes made of leather were not allowed to be inside the house. If someone came to the house with shoes on to visit, shoes were to be left outside before they entered the house.

Grandmother told me that I was so terrified of the dark skinned porter who carried me on his back that throughout the journey, I cried and cried until I fell asleep. I just smiled at this remark not knowing what to say. I admired my grandmother for her courage and determination. Imphal valley is at the radius of 50 miles surrounded by the hills. So to reach anywhere outside Manipur, one has to cross the hills. The first day when they reached the foot hill the last leg on Imphal valley, the golden rays of the setting sun still on the western sky, the traders signaled that it was time to rest before they started climbing up the hill. Most of them in groups cooked their own food and some brought champak (flattened rice), which could be soaked in water and eaten. Those who cooked their meals did so on the makeshift cooking place with three stones raised from the ground. Keeping a fire burning with the collected twigs and pieces of dried tree branches, they cooked rice and lentils. After the meal they made sure that there were no burning twigs or embers left. They poured water over the stones until no trace of fire was left. Resting the night brought them energy to climb the hills for the rest of the day.

Well-rested early in the morning, the leader of the group announced the departure. They started their uphill journey. This was my mother's first travel on foot on the hills and she had only seen the flat land of Imphal. Grandma had gone outside Manipur before on the bus via Dimapur and then by train while travelling on a pilgrimage to Mathura and other holy places with a group of people. They started climbing the slopes of the hills and it was not much of hardship in the beginning in the cool early morning breeze. Once mid-day approached, their climb became steeper making them more and more tired, but for those traders carrying their merchandise it was a routine adventure. When they felt they needed to eat, they had a quick lunch and rested for a short time near a stream. They didn't want to waste much time during the day and hence proceeded toward their destination. The traders usually knew where they could find a good place for their break in the journey. Sleeping at night under the open sky and trekking during day they continued their journey. The leaves of autumn turned completely orange to welcome the cool winter days.

On the third and fourth days, the climbing became more and more steep. Passing through the thick jungles, looking down the steep side of the hill was a frightening sight. One side was a steep hill covered with tall trees with thick bushes and on the other side was a gorge deep down and covered with thickets. Sometime they had to pass under the shadow of the trees and hardly could they see sunshine. Feeling stuffy and hot they continued their journey with bright hope of seeing sunshine soon. They could hear an occasional flutter of frightened birds warning their own species. Once they were out of those thick bushes, they felt as if they were once again on land where human beings could live. When daylight faded into the darkness of the night, they decided to give their aching limbs rest. Cool air soothed their tired limbs and after eating their food, everyone dozed off, welcoming the sweet slumber. Stunningly, the silence of the night brought some uneasy feeling to my grandmother and mother but they had to act brave. The only sound they could hear was the crickets or some other insects and their own breathing sound, also some the tired men's heavy breathing.

On the 10th day of their journey they were near their destination, Jiribam. Impatiently longing to reach their destination, they proceeded slowly downward in their journey toward Jiribam. It was late afternoon when their descending journey started. When the sight of plains of Jiribam came into view my grandmother was thrilled and she was overcome with happiness and joy. Her wish was coming true and her daughter was going to be united with her husband and her granddaughter *with her father. I believe father knew about our arrival at Jiribam from a message sent through earlier traders. I was glad to hear that. At least he was ready to welcome us. Finally my grandmother's wish was fulfilled. After staying for two months in Jiribam, my grandmother returned to Imphal along with another group of traders.*

Now you know that I was born in Imphal, not in Jiribam. One more interesting thing I want you to remember is that the British ruled Manipur only for 100 years compared to rest of India when British ruled for more than 200 years after many years living in India as traders.

Yours lovingly,
Ine

*   *   *

Journal Entry
Lake Tahoe, California
April 16, 2001

Today we all go to Lake Tahoe and stay at Tahoe keys Blvd # 27. Bala, Lall's friend, also came with his wife and their young son. My oldest grandson Dev also invited his friend Cody to join us. The parents take the kids to the snow for skiing while I go to the Harrah's casino. While they are on their way to hiking, I spend most of my time just walking around the lake and enjoy the view. The kids, Lucas, Leon, Dev, Cody are busy at the arcade while I take the opportunity to go to the casino again. I play only five cents and sometimes twenty-five cents on the rollicks. I am so excited when I get a $90.00 jackpot on the five cent rollicks. Altogether I win

$102.00. Not bad, I guess. While Bala with his family drive around the lake we go inside Harrah's and to the 18th floor for lunch at the buffet. On our last day everyone starts missing home food so we cook rice and dal for a change.

Journal Entry
San Ramon
April 20, 2001

We arrive home after encountering heavy snowfall on the way. Luckily our vehicle has four-wheel drive and is good in snow. But Bala's car needed chains and we waited till the chains were hooked in. Then on the way home, we all stopped at the Jelly Belly factory.

Journal Entry
San Ramon
July 2001

Since I started working, I am building up more clients. I meet a lady who hosts Sai Baba's bhajan (weekly prayer and singing) regularly at her home. Since I used to go to Baba's bhajans in Kalikota and Shillong, India before, I gladly join the group and attend regularly. I cannot sing but can join the melodious flow of the tune.

Now I decide to opt out of Soka Gakkai International even though some of the members try very hard to go back to the organization. So I now choose to stay with my original group from India—Sathya Sai Baba religious organization.

*   *   *

Valencia, California
September 10, 1999.

Dear Gojen,

Today, I will continue the story I wrote in my previous letter. Since my grandmother left Jiribam she was always worried about us. So far away and not knowing how my mother and I were doing, she had uneasy feelings. It was my mother's first experience of life together with my father. My mother was always quiet and hardly spoke except when doing the usual house work. She never tried to speak up for herself for

Figure 6 Grandmother RK Sanachubi Devi

anything. But as my dear father was a dominating figure and his temper was always a part of him, my mother did not dare to say anything to him. As I grew up I saw more and more of the dysfunctional situation. While in Imphal, Grandmother saw her younger daughter Ibeyaima, who lived with her husband and mother-in-law, found her to be doing fine. She didn't have to worry about her. Her main concern was about her older daughter, Ibemhal, who was now with her husband in Jiribam. Her strong desire to see us grew more day by day. She also mentioned that she heard some strange stories about our life in Jiribam from people who had visited Cachar and Jiribam.

After about one year, my grandmother Sanachaubi came back to Jiribam to see us. She joined another group of regular traders in the spring of 1937. She walked along the same route with hopes of seeing her daughter and granddaughter, knowing they would be happy to see her again. But it didn't turn out that way. Her expectations turned into a nightmare.

"Ibemhal, I have come to see you."

My mother didn't smile or show any sign of happiness to see her own mother coming back. She didn't utter a single word, only tears trickled from her eyes. It was unbelievable, and turned out to be beyond my grandmother's imaginings.

My mother continued doing her household chores like cooking and other household works. Grandmother saw the difference in her daughter's behavior. It was not like before. She didn't even have any new clothes to wear, only ones Grandma had left when she had left for Imphal. Mother was in a deep depression, which people took as mental illness. To my grandmother's surprise, the baby (me) who was by now nearly two years old, had not started saying a single word. People who took pity on my mother started informing Grandmother about father's affairs and involvement with other women. Mother was there in the house just like a maid who did the chores of household activities. She had suffered alone as she couldn't express to anyone, going into a deep depression. It was now clear why my father hadn't planned to go back to Imphal for his wife and child; he already had a woman as his mistress. To please his mother, father had not objected to the arranged marriage with my mother. As I had mentioned earlier, my mother was left with her in-laws just a few days after the wedding and Father went back to Jiribam to join his work. She stayed with her in-laws nearly one and a half years after the wedding.

I couldn't help but resent my father's actions. Finally my grandmother decided to stay over to sort out what was going on. She took advice and suggestions from people. Sometimes she sought help from local medicine men either with medicines or prayer rituals. That was the only way she could think of helping her daughter return to normal.

My mother became better with the love and care of Grandmother. But something in her spirit was shattered forever. My grandmother's arrival to Jiribam for the second time was a blessing for all of us. The whole atmosphere changed and our lives took a new turn as she decided to stay on for a while to sort out the mess we were in. In her company, I gradually picked up words and spoke. In the following years, my father depended mostly on Grandmother for his social connections with the local people. She was the one who kept in contact with everyone in the neighborhood and our relatives.

Even today, I find myself wishing I had done more to make her happy and hadn't chosen wrong directions that made her sad. But one realizes certain mistakes only late in life. I wish I could turn the clock back and start all over again. I miss her so much. She had to have been an angel on earth for all she did for all of us. Most of the people younger than she called her Aigya to show respect. (It means under your command). She was about 5'1" tall and always had a perfect figure. I never saw her overweight. By the local standard, her complexion could be counted as fair. She was respected by all.

She was always eager to teach me the conventions of her day so that I would grow up a decent girl. Here are some of them:

- *Decent girls don't laugh loudly nor giggle. That's not the way a girl should behave. (I presumed just a smile was enough).*
- *If a woman walks in the house and makes noise with footsteps, the Goddess of Wealth, Laxmi, will be reluctant to enter the house. (I loved climbing trees, running in the fields and walk-skipping. I must have been around 10 years old when Grandmother warned me that I should walk gracefully like a lady. I tried to follow her advice but I always landed myself like a tomboy.)*

- *Don't look straight into a man's eyes. (What an opposite way of doing things. Nowadays we are supposed to look straight in the eyes while talking to show confidence.)*

One thing I surely inherited from my father is my temper. Of course, I grew calmer and more controlled after I got married and more so after my children were grown.

Father missed Grandmother when she passed away on February 10, 1970. I heard him cry one day telling about her contributions to the family. On the day of Grandmother's death I saw the mystery bird come to me in my dream.

The Mystery Dove

> I dozed and dreamt,
> Standing near a Jasmine flower bush,
> Its sweet fragrance rushing into my lungs
> The chilly wind of the dawn
> Flushing on my face.
> I stood in a pensive mood
> As if waiting for someone dear to me.
> A white dove flew over me
> Murmured in a sad melancholy tone
> But clearly,
> "Jamuna, I'm leaving forever"
> I looked up in surprise
> As the white dove passed by me
> Flying slowly, slowly far away
> As it crossed the horizon
> My eyes could no longer hold it.
> It was February 10, 1970

*   *   *

September 9, 2001

I leave for India by United Airlines via Hong Kong on Sept 5th, 2001, and reach New Delhi on the 6th of September. On the 7th, my sister-in-law, Meera, and I go to McDonald's for lunch. An American fast-food in India! We were quite happy to see it. Actually, this fast food chain has become very popular in India. The next day we are on our way to see Dada Anandaram and having lunch with him brings back all our old memories of when his wife Dhuru was still alive.

This visit is to close all of my accounts and I complete other unfinished work. On the 15th of September I leave for Kolkata by Rajdhani (train), paying Rs.1730. The next day, I reach Kalikota and stay at Mamaji's place. Bani Mitra, my nursing college classmate, usually comes to see me, and this time she takes me again to Suruchi, our favorite eating place for Bengali food. Suruchi is run by abused women who are given shelter by the organization.

After I finish all my tasks, I meet my old family friends and relatives. On September 20th, I take Jet Airlines flight 621 via Jorhat and land in Imphal around 2 pm. I am so happy to be in my home town. I see my parent's house where my younger brother Tuleswer and his family live. I look at it with fond memories and move toward the back side where my other brother Irananta has built his house.

On September 29th 2001 we have a reunion lunch with all my old friends in Imphal. Everyone who has been with me sometime or other during my days in school and college is there for this event so nicely organized by my brother Irabanta. One of the ladies is Bimola, who used to be a good friend of mine. She has told me about a Manipuri family living in San Jose, California. I had not known of any Manipuri family in the US. I am so happy when I come to know about Olivia and her husband Sudeep, whose father is Dr. Jatiswer, a doctor who had worked in Imphal Civil Hospital when I was working in the surgical ward.

Leaving for Guwahati to talk to the bank manager does not bring any fruitful result. The lawyer, my husband had engaged takes no interest in my situation. Since Rup passed away, everything seems to be going in the wrong direction. Mr. Cajee, our tenant in the Shillong house, is very nice and helpful but when a chance is in front of him he will naturally take it. Things are not going the way my husband expected when he was alive. The bank has acquired the house and is sold to the present tenant. Everything happens for a reason. I decide not to fuss about it any more. Things would have been different if Rup was still alive. Spending time with my friend Nurara and some other old friends in Shillong has been very pleasant, though.

Figure 7 Our second house, Shillong

October 9, 2001, I leave Shillong for Mumbai where I stay at Gopi and Jairam's place. I have to complete some more work dealing with Rup's accounts. Mohini, my husband's younger sister, has come to see me from Pune and we spend some time together visiting all the relatives including Hiru and her family and Naresh and his family. I return to Delhi on October 14, 2001. After spending about 10 days there I leave for the US on 24th October. It is the best flight for my journey, thanks to Sujan and Paro for their gift of mileage for business class. I reach San Francisco's airport around 8.30 am and am so happy to be back home to my room, my own bed. A time to relax after this long journey.

Previously, I had taken out a business license to work from home as medical transcriptionist. Now that I have changed my mind as signs of carpel tunnel developed in my hand, I cancel it.

* * *

San Ramon, California
January 10, 2000

Dear Gojen,

Do you know I had cousins and they came to Jiribam during the World War ll? That was the best time of my childhood as we had lots of fun together. This was the time India was involved in the fight taking the side of the British and at the same time we were fighting for independence from them. I remember one day my father came back from office in a pensive mood.

My mother didn't want to disturb him and went straight to the kitchen to make tea for him as usual. My grandmother just entered the room from the backyard with some vegetables from our kitchen garden. She had plucked some green leaves to cook for our night meal. She looked at my father and with some concern, asked, "Something is worrying you?"

He nodded. "There was bombing at Imphal town and I hear quite a lot of people died."

"When did it happen?" she was shocked.

All our relatives were in Imphal town. My father's immediate family was there, his mother Leinou and sister, Aunt Pashot, with her two kids at Keishampat. My grandmother's side included her brother and sisters living in Yumnam Leikai, Yaiskul. As there was no contact available everyone was worried.

I left my ragdolls inside the shoe box neatly arranged and hurried toward the adults. I heard all their conversations as I came near my grandmother and stood there listening more closely.

My mother brought tea and snacks for my father and then also stood listening to the on-going conversations. Father said he heard news that the first bombing by the Japanese was on Sunday May 10, 1942 on localities like Khoyathong, Menjorkhul, Thangmeiband, Chingmeirong, Mantripukri at Koirengei airstrip, in the South Palel/Kakching airstrip.

"What about your family there?" Grandmother asked him.

"I am not sure. I believe people are leaving Imphal to take shelter in the villages."

Next day father got the news, Grandmother Leinou and Aunt Pashot were all right and they did not go to the village for shelter. Instead they were planning to come to Jiribam.

"They are on their way. Pashot with her two kids; it may take more days than usual for them to reach here." My aunt's son, Amubi, was nine years old and her daughter, Purnimashi, was seven, the same age I was, just few days older.

My mother turned toward me, "Your cousins are going to be here soon. You will have playmates now."

"When will they arrive?" I was excited to hear this news and prayed for them to arrive here soon.

Then every day I asked my mother, "Are they coming today?"

It was during this time I saw soldiers marching at Jiribam even though we didn't see any combat around Jiribam. Many of the soldiers were Indian, part of the Allied Forces of the British Empire.

As a seven-year-old, I was happy when the soldiers passed by, stopped and talked to me. Almost every day they stopped and asked me many questions. Even though I did not understand everything they spoke, I could understand when they asked my name and my age. I smiled and replied to whatever I understood. I even got a bread loaf from them which was my first taste of bread in my life. We never ate bread at home except our own type of food. Since I was dressed like a boy they presumed that I was a boy.

One day my father said, "Maybe they will be here today." It was the happiest day of my life. I had already waited for so long.

I presume their trip was more than two weeks. Grandma Leinau and Aunt Pashot and her two kids arrived at Jiribam. My uncle, Kulabidhu, my father's youngest brother was also posted in Jiribam in Police Department. He was with his wife and two sons and another cousin—sister Mani, daughter of my middle uncle who passed away very young. Now I had five cousins to play with. My maternal grandmother's sister-in-law (her husband's elder sister) also came to live with us during this time. The bombing continued for two years as inhabitants left Imphal and took shelter at different villages.

So far I had grown up without siblings and with no one to play with, and now I had my cousins. We played a lot. Our favorite game was to climb the grapefruit tree and sit on its branches. We could all sit comfortably and chit chat. Mani, my oldest cousin, was the leader. She used to direct us in what to play. Hide-and-seek was one of our favorite games. Sometimes we skipped ropes. The next door Dak Bungalow guest house was usually vacant and hence we played there most of the time. We made a nice make believe cooking place there and then feast.

Sometimes we played soldiers and pretended to be shooting at each other. Our play battlefield was around the open area in front of our house where I had run often with my kites. While people in Imphal were dispersed and lived as refugees in far away villages, life in Jiribam was different. For me that was the best time of my life when my cousins were around.

The big community pond was the one where all my cousins learned swimming. I was the only one who couldn't learn as my *grandmother Sanachaubi wouldn't allow me to go there. She said there were leeches and she was afraid the leaches may bite me. I wished I could just go into the pond and learn to swim as my cousins did. But I obeyed grandmother and I didn't.*

After sometime my paternal grandmother Leinou started having serious health problems. My father made a wooden back rest as she could not breathe properly while lying down. The medical doctor who was in charge of the district hospital and the only doctor available in that area came to see her. I saw Grandmother Leinou with her swollen feet and came to know she had a heart problem. After about two months of suffering she passed away in this remote countryside. She didn't have a chance to go back to her home town Imphal again. My father performed a grand Sorat (ceremonial dedication to the departed soul) for her and he was very happy that he could do this for her.

After a few months at Jiribam, too, we were given instructions that when the warning siren blew, we were supposed to run to the covered trenches and stay in darkness by turning off all lights. World War all was in full swing after Germany's Adolph Hitler and Mussolini of Italy invaded Europe and Britain. Japanese soldiers were approaching India after taking control of Burma/Myanmar. The British General Stillwell with his troops and missionary nurses walked through the jungles of Burma and reached Imphal after twenty-nine days. Other generals from different parts of Burma also arrived in Imphal, thus completing withdrawal from Burma. The Japanese occupied Burma completely in 1942. The Japanese goal was to capture Imphal and thus to march up to Upper Assam to cut off supplies to China and other parts of Asia.

This was a disaster for the Allies. Control of Imphal became a do or die situation for all sides. The British Army fortified the Imphal plains, making air strips and thus the allies resisted fiercely while the Japanese army attacked continuously. The

Japanese continued bombing Imphal for two years as the war became deadlocked in this town, neither side able to advance. Both forces were fortified with large number of soldiers; the situation was critical.

The American Commando Force was then authorized to serve with General Wingate. Fighting continued in Imphal and the American Project 90752 was drafted. On May 8, 1944 the Third Combat Cargo was created and joined the war. The Japanese lost about 50,000 soldiers fighting in the Bishnupur area of Manipur. They had to retreat as the British and allied forces advanced forward despite the heavy monsoon rains. After six weeks of Japanese invasion, the Imphal plains were rescued on the 16th of November, 1944. The victory in Imphal was a turning point. Lord Mountbatten went to Sylhet personally to thank the American Combat Cargo Group.

In one of my most vivid memories of the war, a group of fighter planes weare flying over our area with a blasting sound. I shuddered at that sound and was scared thinking that any time there could be bombing. By then, my soldier friends could no longer be seen. They had moved on. I hope by the end of the war, they had gone back to their loved ones.

The bombing in Burma and at the eastern border of India forced many people from Burma (mostly of Indian origin) to flee to India. They came walking all the way through the rugged terrain and hills of Burma and Manipur and some of them finally crossed Jiribam on their way to their destinations in India.

By the middle of 1944, the influx of refugees continued in streams and exhausted, many could not make it to their hoped for destinations. Most of the refugees looked haggard; there was a rumor that a child on the roadside was seen suckling the breast of a mother who lay lifeless on the dirt road. WW ll ended after the atomic bomb, "Little Boy," was dropped first on Hiroshima

August 6, 1945, and then three days later on Nagasaki. The rescue of Imphal-Kohima could be described as the Normandy of the East.

After about two years, the condition in Imphal improved and people started returning. My cousin, Mani, also left for Imphal with my uncle's family. My aunt, Pashot, became a second wife as she married Mr. K. Kamini Singh, a famous classical singer who lived in Lakhipur, a village at the neighboring state. He had grown up kids from the first wife, who were very loving and helpful to all of us. Now that my cousins were gone, I was again left all alone.

In 1940 India continued in turmoil, fighting for independence. Gandhi and his 40,000 followers were imprisoned. Gandhi was eventually released from prison in 1945.

The Imphal-Kohima war may be forgotten but two cemeteries bring it to life for many. The Imphal cemetery has 1300 British burials, 10 Canadians, five Australians, 220 Indians, 40 East Africans, 10 West Africans, and 10 Russians. A similar number of soldiers were buried in Kohima. The bronze plaque at the entrance of Kohima cemetery is engraved with these words, "When you go home tell them of us, for their tomorrow we gave our today." These words were found in the pocket of a soldier in World War II (CBI) Theater, April 1942-January 1945 in the seize of Imphal-Kohima, I learned from the writings of Lalit Pukhrambam, PhD

Yours lovingly,
Ine

*   *   *

Journal entry
San Ramon, California
October 30, 2002

I continue to have more clients in the salon and I enjoy working here. I am thankful to God that I still can work in my late s sixties.

Toronto, Canada
November 23, 2002

Arrive at Toronto on 23rd Nov and I stay with Jibesh and Colleen. Next day, on Sunday we go to Colleen's mom's place for her birthday. It is Colleen's baby shower also. Coming back from Toronto to California on November 29, I take a shuttle and Bart train up to the Dublin station; so much walking and the changes in Bart and the shuttle in between make me so tired

*   *   *

San Ramon, California
March 23, 2000

Dear Gojen,

Now is the real family history. Do you remember I wrote you about the Magic Wand and Broomstick? Well, the story after that is here for you to know because you and your cousins are the generations who came from that moment of time.

I already told you that I was really confused and upset when I heard my grandmother asking her friends to look for a bride for my father. We had just accomplished our effort to send Kunjo away. And now Grandmother wanted to find another new wife for my father? I know she wanted someone who could give a son for the family, but I had been getting all the attention and now a child, especially a boy, would take away their love from me. As for my mother, she had become resigned to her fate as she was not having another child.

This was an important period of time for everyone. My grandmother understood my father's interest. To get a suitable girl as a bride for him was the only solution. My moods swung from fretting over her idea to excitement at the idea of having a sibling. But I held a grudge about why girls couldn't be an asset to the family.

My grandmother's search for a bride continued while father patiently waited. Grandma as usual never wavered and kept asking all her friends to find the right bride who would be willing to marry him. Even though most of her friends felt it was odd to look for a bride for her own son-in—law, they also believed that a son for the family was important.

That afternoon on Saturday, I accompanied my grandmother while she visited her friend Leiriksana in Dibong village. We walked on the dirt road from Babupara where we lived. After walking on the dirt lane which led to Dibong village about two miles away from our quarter, passing the Hospital on the hilltop on the left and on the right the huge big mansion of the Magistrate, we reached an area where we didn't see any inhabitants. We saw only thick jungle with trees and bushes. We walked faster so that we could reach the village.

Now in the heat, perspiration dripped from Grandma's face and she wiped it away with the corner of her scarf. I used the corner of my shirt to wipe my dripping perspiration as I didn't have anything like a handkerchief.

After walking a half mile more, we saw village huts all in a row about a quarter mile from the bank of the Jiri River. Those houses had thatch roofs and the walls were plastered with mud on bamboo frames. All the houses were built in the same style and lined the right side of the main path, across paddy fields on the left. The dirt main pathway along the village was raised and was parallel to those huts. One could walk near the houses taking the side lanes and could walk past near the fences to enter someone's house. My grandmother's friend lived almost at the end of Dibong village. We usually used to visit two/three houses whenever we went to the village. That day grandma was interested to go to her friend Leiriksana's house only.

While walking I saw village boys playing on the marshy and muddy field and some tending their buffalos. I was in awe watching how happy they were, playing on marshy land and the dirty water of the pond. It was very amusing when I saw some of the village boys enjoying sitting on the backs of the buffalos. But I didn't see any girls in the open field. They played around their houses and learned how to cook and weave cloths. When they grew up and married, some of them helped male folks working in the paddy field.

All the houses built in the same style were called Yumjau, and usually had a huge long hall, the length being four times more that the width. The whole length was divided with partial partitions and beds placed in a row for each member of the family. The first partition was one for the oldest member of the family and the next ones according to the seniority of the male folk. At the last corner was the cooking area; only the woman who cooked meals could enter the place. Just near the kitchen there was a place known as funga which was the place where fire was kept alive continuously with the help of compacted husks just like we had in our kitchen of the government quarter. The Meities population was predominant in the valley, and comprised of Lamba Sarak village and Dibong village, Kalinagar village and Babupara.

All the houses had their verandah in front. Usually there were two ponds, one for washing and bathing and another pond used for drinking water in the front of a house. But the inhabitants depended mostly on the Jiri River.

The temple for the villagers was located in the middle of the village and near the temple was a big hall where ceremonies like weddings and dance dramas such as for Ras Leela were performed. Among the Meities, Bramhins were the priests who usually performed the rituals. After we had passed almost the whole village, we reached our destination, Leiriksana's house. Just when we pushed open the gate made of bamboo, Leiriksana came out of the house. She smiled and greeted us. Her husband was not at home and their kids who were grown had been out for study at Silchar town in Cachar district. There had been no school in Jiribam until just then when a middle school from first grade to sixth grade was opened.

We finally entered the front yard known as Sumang. At the front verandah, where people were entertained, Leiriksana unrolled a mat made from a local plant something similar to cane. I immediately sat down on the mat as I felt tired from walking. It was a long walk for me.

Leiriksana, a skinny woman, gave me a friendly look and said she was happy to see me. She was taller than my grandmother. Only one common thing was that they both had the last name/title Sana, which meant they were far descendants of royal families. So they both were in the same higher rank in the society's caste system. They could share the same hookah for smoking, which was the privilege for elderly people in those days. If it was some other person belonging to other subcastes, there *would be a twisted cone shape made out of a banana leaf known as Lakkoi to hold the Nganthak, a small container made of pottery clay for the burnt tobacco mixture, which was covered by a piece of burnt ticcki made out of charcoal.*

Along with the hookah to smoke, it was the custom to offer pan (beetle nut and pan leaves). Grandmother's friend brought out the lighted tobacco container hooked on hookah for my grandmother. She started puffing.

"How is everything going?" Leiriksana asked. "Have you heard anything about Kunjo?"

"Nothing, I have no news about her." Grandmother replied. "I hope she does not come back."

I sat listening to their talk; some of it was interesting, and some I couldn't understand. One thing that captured special attention was my grandmother asking again for her friend to look for a bride for my father. I realized that she came to visit her friend for this purpose.

"I think I know someone, a distant relative of mine. But they are in Kamrangkha in Cachar." Leiriksana gave Grandmother the information.

Grandmother's face lit up with renewed interest.

"Oh! It is very good news. When can you find out? We shall talk with the parents," she insisted.

Grandmother explained to me that Kamrangkha was also in Cachar near Lakhipur and that the girl belonged to Raj Kumari (RK—far descendants of Royal families. She was of marriageable age. Grandmother was overjoyed to hear that the girl belonged to the same sub caste title of RK family as hers.

"I can find out and let you know."

"Please send the message as soon as possible and then we can go and talk to her parents." Grandmother insisted again.

"One thing, she is not so good looking." My grandmother was not bothered about her looks. She was happy that the girl

belonged to the RK family. That was the best she wanted in the quality of a girl.

After she puffed her hookah few times, grandmother gave it back to her friend.

"Well, we now want to take leave," and again she reminded her friend, "Please send the message to the girl's parents soon."

She got up from the mat and I followed my grandmother as we left Leiriksana's house and walked back home without visiting anyone else's house. I missed visiting my friend, the daughter of the village's Brahmin family (we used to call each other Itah meaning buddy.) But I kept quiet and didn't want to ask Grandmother anything more. The sky was covered with October clouds. There was no sign of rain, though. And even the clouds didn't help rid the Jiribam foothills of summer heat. I now longed to reach home sooner and sit under our hand-pulled fan or swing under my grapefruit tree.

About a month passed. Leiriksana sent a message for my grandma. "The girl's father will be visiting her house next Monday." That would be in five days.

She wanted my grandmother to meet him. Grandmother immediately talked father about it and he was ready and he had no objection to that proposal. Only they had to wait to hear confirmation from the girl's father.

When the girl's father came, the elders met and talked things over. Everything was settled and agreed upon. A date for the betrothal was fixed. An exchange of kabok (a kind of sweet made with puffed rice and jaggery) and fruits was done as the engagement before the official nuptial took place.

At the end of September 1946, we all had to go to Kamrangkha via Lakhipur. We stayed overnight at Aunt Pashot's house and next day we had to proceed walking to girl's village. I was given a ride on the bike of Birendra Singh, step-son of Aunt Pashot. He was always ready to help us.

It was a short ceremony known as kanya katpa (for becoming husband and wife). Usually a wedding ritual was not performed in the way they had agreed beforehand between the two parties. After the short ceremony Tamphasana, the bride became my father's wife. Even though the girl was very ordinary in looks there were other qualities. She was young and vibrant, the main reason being, she belonged to the RK family. After the ceremony we left for Jiribam with the new bride. This time we didn't follow the original path. We took a short dirt road through the hills reaching Jiribam directly without going via Lakhipur. It was a shorter way but through the winding muddy path on the hills through the bushes and trees. I remember water trickling from the side of the hill and in some places leeches hanging around on the side branches of the bushes. I even imagined a ghost hanging around. The bride walked, too, accompanied by her brother Herangoisana. He was also moving with us to start his business as a tailor. He carried his sewing machine on his shoulder. As Jiribam did not have a tailor, my grandmother had convinced him and his family to have his business in Jiribam.

As for my mother I could sense my mother's feelings; even though she was sad she had to resign to her fate. It was always the woman who was to be blamed if she couldn't conceive and unable to give a son.

We reached Jiribam after walking a whole day. My father and the bride were given a room for the honeymoon night inside the main house. With the hope of getting a son for our family, life continued as usual at Jiribam. Now you know the real history!

Yours lovingly,
Ine

* * *

Journal Entry
San Ramon, California
November 30, 2000

Today after I came across an animal begging for food in
the backyard of our house, I was tempted to write a letter to
my childhood pet Nilu.

Dear Nilu

*I was ten when I met you and fell in love with you instantly.
It was the day I accompanied my grandmother while visiting
someone in Kalinagar village. You immediately captured my
attention. You were so tiny and cute and playful.*

*I still remember that on the way to Kalinagar just at the side
of the sugar cane field something was going on. We could smell
something sweet and tingling hitting our nose. Grandmother
asked me, "Do you want to drink something sweet?"*

"I don't know. Is it good?"

"You can try."

*So we turned toward the shade where the villagers were busy
making brown sugar from sugarcane juice. Inside the ditch, logs
of woods were kept burning. On top of the fire was a large tin
container for boiling the sugarcane juice until it was solidified
into jaggary (a brown colored sugar). A woman among those
villagers handed me an earthen cup containing the hot sugarcane
juice. It was very good.*

*Then when we came toward Tomba's house, we passed
your gate and saw you following Moina the girl who had just
gotten water from the pond in front of her house. (Moina had
the hairstyle of bangs on her forehead and on two sides of her
cheeks, chin-length hair. That was the sign in those days to show
that the girl was now of marriageable age.) Having just finished*

filling her pitcher with water, she was ready to go inside her house. My grandmother called her name.

"Moina, how are you doing?"

Moina turned and smiled and answered. "Oh, where are you going, Aigyabok?" she asked, responding to my grandmother. Aigyabok (grandma with respect.)

"We are going to Tomba's house. We're wondering about that little thing following you."

"Yes, I found it when it was very small and lost its parents."

"So cute," I said.

Moina then asked me, "Do you want to have it?" I couldn't believe my ears.

"Yes, yes," I shouted with excitement and looked at my grandmother anxiously waiting for her response. She seemed surprised at the unexpected outcome. Its lovely, fluffy tail still waving, it stood near Moina. So friendly, it let me put my hand on her and feel the softness. Grandmother was still thinking and not responding. I looked at her begging to allow me to take it home. Then she finally asked Moina, "What do you feed a squirrel?"

"Give her some corn and nuts, also fruits."

Later we came to know Moina the girl who took care of you was to be married soon. So she wanted you to have someone else who could take care of you. She put you in your wooden box with some rags in it for you to sleep. You didn't cry or try to run away. Your fur so soft and fluffy tail, how I enjoyed touching them. You didn't mind and played with me. After that day, you were my constant companion for nearly a year.

It was seven decades ago that I lost you one day without any warning. The terrible day you were crushed under the foot of the 180 lb weight of our dear guest. He was unaware of your habit of following people in the house and he stepped on you accidentally. I cried for days never forgot you. This year 2012, during the winter months, a couple of squirrels made their nest between the roof and ceiling of our house facing the backyard by bringing all the strings from the nylon outdoor umbrella and turning them into pieces for their nest. One of the couple always stood looking toward our kitchen expecting food, because we had stopped leaving out birdseed. It stood as if asking us why there were no birdseeds. We felt pity on it and gave it cashew nuts and ground nuts, and it became a regular waiting schedule, sometimes even knocking on the glass door. When spring came it disappeared suddenly and never came back.

I feel sad again at the memory of losing my beloved Nilu of my childhood days. So this letter is to let you know that I always miss you and never forget you, my beloved.

Your last keeper,
Jamuna

*   *   *

Journal Entry
Imphal, India
April 5, 2003

Today I'm visiting my brother Irabanta after his wife's passing. I really miss my sister-in-law Shanti. She was my confidant and friend. In the evening I went to see Mr. Narayan Sharma who was in his bed sick and lonely. He was a very talented figure in Manipur for his contributions to the Manipuri film industry. When I came back home Dr. Prmchand was waiting to see me with some of his friends. One of them is a very old friend whom I have not seen for years. It is so nice to see an old friend without any notice giving me a surprise visit. The only thing I couldn't understand is why he gets up suddenly and storms out to the door, his friends following him like military commandoes. I just couldn't help but be amused.

*   *   *

San Ramon
May 19, 2000

Dear Gojen,

It was the happiest day for everyone when my brother Irabanta was born on November 29, 1947. Our life as a family seemed complete. At this time my grandmother's wish to get my father transferred back to Imphal was finally coming through. In January 1948 father came back from work and announced, "Guess what? I have got a letter for a transfer and I can join the excise department in Imphal!"

We were all very happy and surprised and my grandmother was exceptionally happy. That news was long awaited one as my admission in Imphal School was granted; it was the right time for this news to come.

I had though just found a friend, the girl whose father was newly posted as Magistrate in Jiribam. She was same age as I was. A few months back, my grandmother had asked me to join her in visiting the new magistrate. I was happy I went. The Magistrate's daughter and I became very good friends.

That day I had put on my green frock, which had bold pink flower designs. I usually wore shorts and a shirt like a boy. My parents loved to dress me up as boy. Maybe since they had been longing for a boy, dressing me up to be one was a second best. But this day I decided to wear my frock. My grandmother, Sanachaubi, was particular about how I parted my hair, so I let her do it. She took out one bottle of scented coconut oil and poured a little on her palm. She rubbed the oil in between her palms and then applied the oil on my hair, brushing it in with her fingers.

I waited for her sitting on my swing and after some time I saw her coming out wearing a light colorcotton shawl over her off-white dress called a phanek (long and a innaphi (broad scarf) covering the upper part of the body. (Our local dresses are quite different from in the rest of India. Like in Punjab, a woman's dress is the salwar kamiz, which is different from the rest of India's long wrap-up dresses known as sarees.)

Grandma was slightly taller than five feet. At ten-years-old, I was much shorter than that. She pulled her black hair straight back and made into a knot like a bun. Her face was slightly round with a broad forehead; my mother didn't resemble her except in height. The only other similarity between them was that they were both very calm and poised.

I came to know from my grandmother that my father did not pursue further studies after high school. And it was some sort of exile for him to be posted at this remote place permanently because he had fallen into bad company with a gambling habit that ultimately contributed to the dwindling of our family's wealth. Now his childhood friend, G K Singh, was his boss in the civil office.

In the afternoon my mother usually sat at her loom weaving and this day too she was doing the same while my new mother Imashi Tamphasana stood watching us walk on the lane leading toward the magistrate's house. When I looked back, I saw Imashi Tamphasana turn toward the door, go inside and shut the door behind her.

I walked along with my grandma for some time and then decided to go ahead of her. So I quickened my steps and climbed and jumped on roadside rocks and then waited for her. The gentle breeze blowing made us slightly cooler than usual. Red, white and blue wildflowers greeted us along the path. Those wild flowers fluttered under the blue sky with the gentle blow of the wind creating a spectacular scene. The one I plucked didn't have a pleasant smell, though, and I threw it away. Reflections of the setting sun on the stream and the orange color covering the western sky behind the hills was another view I won't forget. As flocks of birds flew across the sky overhead, I wondered about their destinations. I imagined them flying sometimes above the clouds far away somewhere.

Figure 8 Jamuna and Binodini in 1948

At the end of the lane connecting the main road toward the market, green mangoes hanging from the branches of the trees caught my attention. I wished I could grab some of the mangoes but they were high up. Just after crossing the main street we reached the gate of the magistrate's mansion. There was no guard those days. Grandma pushed open the gate and we could walk in straight to their house. The magistrate's mansion was a huge one. We walked for about three hundred yards toward the bungalow and then took the side entrance. Once inside the side gate we saw six or seven wide steps up leading toward the door facing the eastern side of the bungalow. We looked up toward a room that was wide open and saw the magistrate's family members sitting there. They also saw us. The lady of the house, a woman in her late forties, came toward the door and welcomed us. The second lady who might have been in her early twenties stood behind her smiling. She was very fair and had a very wide charming smile. I could see their daughter inside still standing and watching us. Then she came toward the door but still standing behind the two ladies. She was not so fair in complexion but pretty and had long black thick hair which fluttered below her knees. She stood there with a faint smile like a beautiful rose bud starting to open. I was sure she must be same age as I

"Welcome, please come inside," the older lady said.

My grandmother introduced herself and then me. The ladies looked very happy to see us as we were from the same place, Imphal, and also spoke the same language. The older lady guided us to sit on the cane chairs with cushions. My grandmother sat down and pointed me to sit on one of the chairs. Family members took the other chairs while Binodini still stood nearby. Binodini and I were introduced to each other and her mom asked, "Binodini, would you like to show your friend the new records and listen to those new songs?"

I was a bit shy but still I was interested to watch the gramophone they had and listen to the new Manipuri song which had just come out. It was sung by Ngangbam Nimai Singh, "Jati Kaobi Sakhenbi." My father had a collection of all the Bengali songs, but he had not got the Manipuri language songs as yet.

I waited for her to say something and then finally Binodini said, "Come, we will go to the other end of the room. The gramophone is there." I followed her and sat on the chair near the table. She pulled the stool which was lying nearby for herself. After she opened the gramophone and took out the records, she selected the particular Manipuri song.

"I have never heard any song in Manipuri before. My father always plays Bengali songs." I remarked.

"Yes, it is new; we have just gotten it. Binodini spoke softly, and had a calm, confident bearing beyond her age. Being in the same room we could still see and hear the elders' conversation.

That day I came to know that Binodini was home-schooled as she couldn't attend school during the WWII bombings at Imphal. I was lucky to be in Jiribam where I could attend our newly established school and be away from war-torn Imphal.

"This one is the first Manipuri song," Binodini commented while placing the record on the gramophone to play.

The excitement was unbearable as I heard the song for the first time in our own language. We both were absorbed in the music. Then I saw Ibetombi, the younger lady, go out of the room toward the kitchen perhaps, to instruct their cook to make tea for us. The magistrate's family had helpers to take care of their daily household work. So the two ladies had not much to do except supervise them.

"She is my youngest sister, married to our husband just before we left Imphal. I had to request my sister to marry my husband for the sake of giving a son for the family." As the older lady narrated her story, I saw my grandmother nodding her head in approval. At the kitchen the cook was instructed to make tea which was usually made by boiling water with tea leaves until the color turned dark. Then milk and sugar were added and also a few cardamom pods for extra flavor. When there was good color and aroma, the tea was strained with a strainer into the individual china cups. The cook brought in the tea and some snacks in a round tray. When the cook left, Binodini's mother continued to tell her story. After the birth of their daughter, Binodini, she could not have any more babies so there was no chance for her to give her husband a son.

As I heard their conversation, our own family history came alive. She got her sister while my grandmother got the girl from Cachar. The music was no more charming for me. An uneasy feeling came from thinking about why girls can't be an asset to their families. Binodini didn't look like she was bothered.

"That was the right thing." My grandmother agreed. And then she continued to tell her side of story. "I had to arrange a young wife for my son-in-law so that he could have a son. The girl is from a neighboring district in Assam state." Binodini's mother called us to join them for the tea and snacks.

"Do you want to listen to more songs later on?" my new friend asked me.

"Not today, next time." I replied while picking up one of the biscuits from the dessert plate. I took a small bite and sipped the aromatic cardamom filled tea cup slowly, all the while my mind shrouded with my sentiment. "I will be different," I told myself, a silent pledge. Why can't a girl be an asset to the family? I kept this deep inside me.

When my baby brother Irabanta was born November 29, 1947, I felt the shifting of everyone's attention and I had a bit of jealousy but ultimately I did feel the joy of having a sibling after 11 years.

This is also the year Gandhi began the "March for Peace" in East Bengal, now known as Bangladesh.

Yours lovingly
Ine

*   *   *

Journal Entry
Kauai, Hawaii
June 15, 2003

I took my flight on June 10, 2003 from Oakland airport to Honolulu then to Lihue airport on Kauai Island. Staying for two nights at Kauai Coconut Beach Hotel was so much fun. Walking barefoot on the sand and deep in and waiting for the waves to push through my legs is unforgettable. I also joined the local tour by bus for the Kauai's town of Waimea. The Waimea canyon's rough-cut red rock is a special attraction. It is considered as the Grand Canyon of the Pacific

On 12 June, Nancy, one of the members for the retreat picked me up to go to Camp Slogged in the Mountains. For the Tai Chi Chih retreat we were 12 members. Seven members are from New Jersey and New York, one is from Alaska, one from New Orleans, one from New Mexico, and only I am from California. Six of them are certified trained tai chi teachers and the rest of us are students. We are having training twice a day, one in the mornings and another in the evenings and two campfires.

Today, I leave Kauai before everyone else, as I am booked for an earlier flight.

*   *   *

San Ramon, California
February 2004

Suguna, one of my friends takes me to a driving range and I am introduced to golf for the first time. I start golf lessons from Dale Bradly and still can't swing my club properly. It has become a challenge for me to swing so I can play in the green.

June 6, 2004

Today I receive email from Dr. Premchand that Gojen and his wife are fine and she is very smart. My brother, Irabanta, has stopped drinking. That is a very good news to me.

July 5, 2004

I received my yearly work assessment from Caroline, our manager. Overall it is good.

September 11, 2004

I have lunch at the Human Chinese restaurant with Suguna and Kalpana, who are my clients at the JCPenney Hair Styling Salon. First time she asks me to go to their house, which is in a ranch and has a lovely location in Pleasanton, CA. The beautiful location reminds me of my days at our house in Shillong, India. We all go to Berkeley to do some shopping at the Indian Sari House on Washington Blvd.

September 16, 2004

For Lucas' and Leon's birthdays, I give each of them cash as gifts. We have a BBQ at home to celebrate the birthdays. We have our family and friends over for their birthday party.

September 30, 2004

My entries from this date have been all about my work and a miracle inspired by Dr. Wayne Dyer's book, *Power of Intention.* I had stopped writing to Gojen. So I must start writing today again. Went to Santa Cruz Beach hotel for our family friend, Sujan's, birthday party. It was a nice beach but as usual the water was cold.

I book an Alaska cruise with Bonnie, who is my friend from JCPenney. The cruise is to start on May 16, 2006 from San Francisco.

*   *   *

San Ramon, California
September 12, 2000

Dear Gojen,

Since Binodini and I became good friends, we saw each other every day. I always visited their bungalow as it was spacious and also both her mother and stepmother (aunt) had time for our card game. In my house either my mother or stepmother was busy cooking or doing household chores while my grandmother was always engaged weaving at the loom. The days of my kite flying were gone. I was more inside the house hanging with Binodini and her family playing cards. We usually played by making the sequence of seven of the same card type to show the players and become the winner. (I think it was known as Rummy) We played almost every day after my school. Even my father teased me one day when I returned home after our game. "My gambler daughter has come back!" I just smiled and did not take it seriously. Some days I did not go as I had to do lots of homework, and Binodini said she missed me a lot.

That was the time I was finishing sixth grade and there was no other school to go for 7th grade. Going to Imphal for studies was the only possible way to continue. But there was no chance my parents would send me alone to live with a relative. Luckily my father got the transfer order just in time so that I could take admission for 7th grade in Tamphasana Girls High school in Imphal. But we didn't have a place to live except the plot of land which was inherited by my father as ancestral property in Keishampat. My grandmother's family in Yumnam Leikai was kind enough to let us live with them until we built our house on my father's plot of land at Keishampat.

It was the beginning of 1948 when we were in the final stages of packing for our move to Imphal. Leaving Jiribam was okay with me but leaving my friend Binodini was sad beyond my imagination. The only consolation was that we would meet again once her father was transferred after completing his three-year term. I went to see Binodini the day before we left to say good bye to her.

"Binodini, I hope to see you in Imphal." My voice was partly chocked inside, my tears welling and dripping slowly down. She picked up the corner of her scarf and rubbed her eyes. We couldn't say anything more but we both knew how we felt.

Leaving my favorite grapefruit tree was also painful. But it was something I couldn't help. I bid goodbye to my grapefruit tree as we walked down the street, all of my family members, my grandmother walking beside me. I remembered leaving ten paise inside the house and I felt like going back to get it. But my grandma said no as it was left behind for God and He would bless us on our journey. With those ten paise, I could get a good quantity of my favorite sweetened puffed rice. Since grandma said so, though, it must be what was necessary to do. We passed my friend's place and I looked to see if she was out on the front verandah. She wasn't and she would have come out if she knew we were passing by.

After about a thirty minutes walk, we reached the bank of the Jiri River. I found it quite interesting to see a covered boat as I had never seen one before. We all could fit in comfortably and there was a sleeping arrangement on the floor of the boat with mattresses. My mother, grandma, and stepmother with my baby brother and father all got in. We went downstream and reached Silchar in, may be about 24 hours I presume. Being on my first long journey by boat, I couldn't help but be filled with excitement. The scenic view all along the river cruise was something I could treasure forever in my memory. The open blue sky above and the green vegetation all along the banks of the river provided moments of fascination. Often there was no sign of human settlement. As the sun went down, stars in the clear sky seemed to gather to say farewell to us. The vastness of the water at the confluence of the Jiri River and the Borak River at Cachar was spellbinding. We continued through the Borak River and reached Silchar town.

Once we reached Silchar and disembarked, we headed for the railway station. We took the train from Silchar to Dimapur, another overnight journey. Birendra, my aunt Pashot's stepson had arranged for booking the seats on the train and helped us board. Only my father and grandmother had been on a train before, Grandmother during pilgrimages after her husband's death. Travelling by train seemed frightening after what had happened after the partition of India and Pakistan when riots started between Hindus and Muslims. When India and Pakistan became independent in August of 1947, Jawaharlal Nehru became the first prime minister of India and Jinnah the first prime minister of Pakistan, an Islamic state. In January 1948, Mahatma Gandhi was assassinated and people were mourning the loss of this international figure. He was admired by people for his satyagraha (fasting until death in support of demands for the welfare of the community) and peace march. Living in Jiribam we didn't know much about the effects of the partition. But I am sure my mother and Grandma were not aware of what was happening in the rest of India and the world.

After reaching Dimapur we had to spend one night there. The dinner we had in one of the Manipuri hotels was sumptuous. I still remember the steaming hot rice served with lentil curry, fried fish, and fish curry, and a special dish known as ironba which had ingredients like a most spicy hot red pepper mixed with vegetables and special fermented fish known as Ngari. I had not developed the taste of hot pepper and hence all the adults were the ones who enjoyed it. It is a side dish though.

It was about a seven hours drive through the hills on the Imphal/Kohima Road. The bus stopped at Kohima for about half hour and the view of the small hill town was lovely. I wished we could walk around but our bus had to leave soon. We reached Mau, the border town between Manipur and Nagaland by lunch time. The bus stopped there for about an hour and we had chance to eat a hot lunch cooked and served by the Manipuri Bramhins. This place became our regular place for lunch on our way from Dimapur to Imphal when my husband and I lived in Dimapur for two years while he was having his supply work to the government of Nagaland.

After lunch in Mao we proceeded toward Imphal, and just before reaching the town I saw the valley of Imphal for the first time from the descending hill road before the village of Kangpokpi. We passed the village of Sakami, famous for brewing strong local liquor. The happiness I felt was overwhelming when our destination was nearing and the long journey was soon to *be over. I had read a book once by a British author, in which he offered the description, "Imphal is the Switzerland of the East."*

Yours lovingly,
Ine

*   *   *

Journal Entries
San Ramon, California
January 30, 2005

I receive the gift of a brand new Nissan Sentra fully paid for by my daughter Shobha and my son-in-law Lall. What a surprise! I am so excited.

March 2, 2005

I go to have my mammogram done and the result means I must go again to confirm the result. There is nothing to worry about, my doctor confirms, but I must check again in six months.

August 11, 2005

Visiting Social Security to find out if my 40 units of work contribution to the government, I come to know that by August 2006 I shall get my social security benefits. I am happy that my retirement is coming soon. As I have been working for the last five years at JCPenney I get a wrist watch from the company as a gift.

October 13, 2005

At 8:30, I join the Senior Center's trip to Yosemite along with Bonnie. We have lunch at the Pea Soup Restaurant on the way. Once we reach Yosemite, we are taken by tram for view of the scenic valley of Yosemite. We see people climbing the half dome and it is so exciting to watch the adventures of people around. Have our supper at Ahwahnee Hotel and it is good.

We leave for Hotel Chukchansi on our way back and we all try our luck at the Casino. But I have no luck. Then we have dinner at the hotel restaurant. Bonnie has a stomach problem and diarrhea. Luckily I have some medicines for the journey and give her the anti-diarrhea tablets.

Yosemite, California
October 14, 2005

We leave at 10 am and reach Hilmar Cheese factory around 12 noon. This factory supplies cheese all over California and sends it to other states, too. We have a tour of the factory and purchase one bottle of honey wine and one cheese packet. We reach the Senor Center around 4 pm.

*   *   *

San Ramon, California
January 27, 2001

Dear Gojen,

In February, 1948 after we reached Imphal we were given a place to stay in Yumnam Leikai where my grandmother's brother and his family lived. We had to stay there until my father finished building our house at Keishampat. That part of my life was one of the very best. That locality was known as Ningthem Macha Kollup.

I came across some girls and became good friends; all were of my own age group. We were seven of us and met almost every day after school. I was in 7th grade whereas most of them were in fifth grade but that didn't make much difference; we got along very well. Three girls, Noni, Chaubi, and Nungshi, were from Karam kollup. At Ningthemmacha Kollup there were three of us: Nungshi Sana, Lairen Sana and me. At the temple complex of the Bramhin family there was one girl of the same age whom we called Bamon Ibemma. So we seven girls became inseparable friends during that time.

We used to get together at the temple area often and played longer on weekends. Very soon the festival of color was coming. I could experience the festival in Imphal for the first time as I hadn't had this experience in Jiribam. It is still the most popular festival in Manipur. Holi, known locally as Yaoshang, is celebrated for five days. The first day of the Holy festival is on a full moon around March.

A temporary hut was built by the men folk of the locality on the full moon day, in the open space known as Lai Sumang (every colony had one open space with a temple for the Goddess of Nature from pre-Hinduism). By evening when the moon rose on the eastern horizon, the idol of Lord Mahprabhu was brought from the temple by a priest, who performed the rituals of prayer and singing. Finally, after songs of dedication and aarti (a prayer song dedicated at the time of closing prayer) to the Lord were offered, the idol of Lord Mahprabhu was taken back to the temple, and the hut was burnt down. Once the fire was lit, the children started running to every house for the collection of money just like children run for candy on Halloween's Trick or Treat in the US.

We formed two groups to go to all the houses of the colonies nearby to collect our share of money. We got all together about Rs 4.30 (Rupees four and thirty paise) which was a big amount in those days. We had five days more to collect money. Then depending on the amount of money collected we would have a feast with entertainment like Thabal Chongba (dancing in the moonlight) as well as open air drama in the same open space Lai Sumang.

The next day we all got to play with color. Using either colored water or dry powder, we were ready to splash color onto anyone, even unknown persons. No one could be excused, although today people may ask to be excused. After we mixed our

color in a bucket, we played around the neighborhood throwing colors to each other and to anyone we saw, even women who hid themselves, as we managed to get them out and cover them with color. After we had fun playing with colors till lunch time we all returned to our homes. We had ourselves a good bath taking off all the colors from our body and hair.

Figure 9 Seven friends at Yumnam Leikai

We met again in the afternoon and planned to collect money from the passersby on the street and on the main road. Blocking the streets with rope and stopping mostly young men and passing cycles and vehicles (very few) was another method we had fun indulging in. One smart girl was assigned to collect the money from those we held; they could not go ahead unless they handed over some money. The young men seemed to enjoy the game. The smart girl could get money from them without hesitation. Since there were few vehicles then, it was not a difficult job. (It would be impossible now as the roads are crowded beyond imagination).

On the fifth day the festival, we counted the money and it was Rs 80 and some paisa, a big amount in those days. So now we could celebrate with Thabal Chongba, also one open air drama. Over and above that, we could have a grand feast for ourselves.

For the feast, we engaged a cook, usually of the Brahmin, to prepare our dishes. This is the picture taken in 1948 during the festival of color. I am second from the left in the front row along with my other six friends.

Just after the festival of color we had to move to our house at Keishampat. Once we settled down, I found new friends; some of the girls from our Keisham Leikai attended the same Tamphasana High School. Damayanti in Thiam Leikai our neighbor colony was in the same class and hence we became very close friends.

I met my cousin sister Ibechaubi for the first time in Imphal. She was the child of my aunt Ibeyaima, my mother's younger sister, who died a few years after her daughter was born. My cousin Ibechaubi was stunningly beautiful. She had flawless skin and beautiful features whereas I was skinny and did not have smooth skin like her. Whenever we walked together, anyone passing by would stop and inquire about her identity. I felt myself like a discarded doll. But I was happy that I was in school while she never attended school. Since she didn't have her mother she was brought up by her paternal grandmother. She was not lucky enough to have a normal father as he was mentally unbalanced due to the shock his wife's death. My cousin grew up as a charming and beautiful girl, and many proposals came for marriage. Finally she got married to a Rajkumar (descendants of royal family) boy who was an only son and lived with his mother.

Her mother-in-law always loved her and admired her beauty. But luck didn't give her a long happy married life as her life was cut short while giving birth to her second child. After the death of Ibechaubi her mother-in-law became depressed. She eventually managed to get her son married again to bring up his two small kids and then after a few months, she passed away in her sleep. I still miss my cousin who died so young without seeing her children grow up. I'm grateful that I had a father who was a sole provider for the family and never left us in spite of all his shortcomings. He gave me education and that was the best thing I got from my father.

The important family history was the birth of my brother, (your father) Irabanta on 29 November, 1947.

Yours lovingly,
Ine

*   *   *

Journal Entries
Regal Princess Alaskan Cruise
May 26, 2006

Leaving with Bonnie my friend for a cruise on the Regal Princess from San Francisco. After Lall and Shobha drop us off at Pier 35, we board the ship by 1 pm and have lunch at Lido on the #12 deck. Then we go around to see if there is any show going on and peep into the gift shops for souvenirs. After spending some time in the casino and losing money, we come back to our room.

May 27, 2006

We are still at sea cruising along the coast of Oregon and Washington State. I feel sea sickness, drowsiness. After Dramamine tablets and napping for some time, I feel better. This part of the sea is rough and almost all the passengers are affected. This Saturday evening we have our formal dining.

May 28, 2006

Sunday our time is put back one hour and we find the sea calmer. After breakfast on the 12 deck, I go jogging on the 14th deck.

May 29, 2006

We reach Sitka, a small town in Alaska around 11:30 am. We have to take the ship's tender to the main island and take free buses to the town. Snow capped Mt. Edgecumbe is across the water. After we purchase some gifts and a special angel for Caroline, my manager at salon, we return around 5:30 pm. On the tender ride, we see a whale catching fish.

May 30, 2006

Reach Haines at 7:30 and we go out around 10.30 am. Bonnie and I take a ferry to go to Skagway and walk around Skagway's downtown. Leave Haines at 7 pm. Haines is supposed to be the home of Shilkat bald eagle.

May 31, 2006

Reach Tracy Arm fjord around 7:30 and see icebergs in different colors and sizes: grayish, bluish, whitish. Once we pass through the S shaped water way, the view of the glacier is astonishingly beautiful. Then the ship turns back to go to Juneau, and we see some sea lions sleeping on the icebergs. This whole water way is a breathtaking and cannot be missed.

Arrive at Juneau around 3:30 pm. The next day after breakfast we go out for a tour by helicopter, which drops us at the site of the North Star glacier and the base where dogs are trained for sledging. The camp is usually during May to September. There are usually eight dogs to pull a sledge with a guide and three tourists, two standing and two sitting. The view from the top of the mountain we see from helicopter is so different from all the pictures we had seen before. Leaving Juneau at 1pm for Victoria. On the way again we see whales catching fish.

June 3, 2006

Reach Victoria and we take a Greyline bus to the town. Take a city tour of the different sections of the city, including the castle of the famous Bucharest Garden of Victoria designer and the upscale harbor area.

June 4, 2006

Coming back on the coastal line of Washington State, Oregon, and California we reach San Francisco around 6 am. By the time we get our luggage and come out to wait for our town car, it is almost 9 am. We don't see the car. Hence we call the driver and find that he has been waiting for us to call him. We are relieved that it turns out to be just a miscommunication.

* * *

San Ramon, California
March 2, 2001

Dear Gojen

On day in 1948 at Keishampat, Imphal, my grandmother Sanachaubi, who had just finished her prayer after her bath, a daily ritual in the morning, interrupted me as I was doing my homework. She came inside and stood near me.

"I'll be going to the Mahabali Temple. Do you want to come?" she asked very softly. I was not sure I wanted to go or not. I just looked at her not answering.

She sensed my indecisiveness and said, "Wari leeba (story telling) session is going on in the Mahabali temple hall; it is about Ramayana."

Wari leeba time was always a favorite one for me and Ramayan (a sacred mythological scripture of the Hindus) was the main attraction for me. Now that my interest was suddenly aroused I was ready to go. These professional story tellers of Manipur always made the story very interesting. I came to know that the event was going on for some time and this week was a continuation of ones we had missed. I immediately closed my book.

"What time do we have to leave?"

"We still have more than an hour; if you want to come, get ready soon. We can leave within 30 minutes." I tried to hurry as I didn't want to miss

Figure 10 Idol of Hanumaji and monkeys waiting for fruits

any part of the story. I believe the session was for another one week.

While I was getting ready my grandmother plucked some marigold flowers from the front yard of our house which is just behind the bamboo trees. Those days those bamboos used to give some sort of privacy to our house. Nowadays nothing of the sort is seen.

After flowers filled a basket in a nice arrangement for the deity, she was ready to go to the temple.

The autumn was just approaching and the bright orange marigold flowers were the products of the season from our yard. We got out of the house at 11: 30 am and reached the temple within a half-hour. It was fun to walk, as the roads were empty and there was no traffic congestion. As we approached the dirt road after walking the main road and nearing the temple we saw some monkeys were just sitting in the sun and cleaning lice and insects from their bodies while some others were ready to snatch fruits from those women who had fruits in their hands. I clung tight to my grandmother as I was afraid of these monkeys who were ready to snatch away fruits.

Near the gate there were three women selling fruits and kabok, a sweetened puffed rice, kwai and pan. We purchased a bunch of bananas from one in the middle and walked past toward the temple holding a stick to frighten those monkeys. We actually purchased those bananas to feed the monkeys after we finished our worship inside the temple. As we entered the temple the towering figure of Hanumanji overwhelmed me. The priest, also called Pandit by local people sitting there, did the ritual for us and put red sindoor on our foreheads. The sindoor on the forehead is a symbol of God's blessings. Upon leaving, we fed those bananas to the monkeys assembled in the enclosure. Then we headed towards the big hall where the story session was to begin.

We sat on one of the mats at the front on the women's side of the hall, waiting for Mr. Sumangal Singh, the famous professional storyteller, to arrive. After about five minutes, he arrived on his bicycle. In those days, having a bicycle was as empowering as owning a car is to us today. Everyone was eager to listen to Mr. Singh's stories and he was usually booked six months ahead. He took his seat on his mat in the middle of the open hall facing the audience and paid homage by bowing to the audience just before he started his story session.

Today he began the story from the sacred Hindu scripture of Ramayana where he had left off the day before. The younger brother of Lord Rama, Lakshman lay on the floor unconscious due to an injury from a poisonous arrow shot from the enemy

front of Ravana, the king of Sri Lanka. The poison from the
enemy's arrow could be removed only by the king of Sri Lanka's
Vaidya (head medicine man)

Lord Rama, with his consort Sita and his brother Lakshman,
had left the palace in Oyudha a few years before to keep the
promise made by his father to his third wife Kaikayi. The promise
was to grant a wish when she needed one. Now she wanted her
own son Bharot to rule the kingdom while the brothers were sent
to wander through the country for 12 years.

After walking on foot through the forests and jungles for
many years they spent some time in a hut in the southern part
of India. During that time, Sita was kidnapped by the King
of Sri Lanka while both the brothers were engaged in chasing
golden deer. After the incident, war followed and Hanuman,
the monkey and devotee of Rama, became a part of Rama's
contingent of army. This day, Rama sat near his brother holding
his hand. He was deep in thought as to how to get the Vaidya,
who was a local medicine man, from the kingdom of the enemy
to remove the poison from the piercing arrow on Lakshman's
body. The emotions and actions portrayed by Sumangal had the
audience taking out their handkerchiefs to dry tears. I sobbed
along with the rest of them.

Hanuman was aware of his Lord's predicament. He was
ready to risk going to the enemy's territory and to bring the
Vaidya with him. Even though Rama warned of the danger of
this mission, Hanuman insisted his request be accepted. In the
end, with the blessings of his Lord, Ram Hanuman ventured
toward Sri Lanka on his mission.

He reached Sri Lanka in pitch dark so that no one knew of
his presence there. When he reached the place, the Vaidya was
asleep on a charpoy, (a light frame with ropes woven across to
sleep on). Praying with his Lord's name, Hanuman slowly picked
up the charpoy along with the Vaidya. And he flew back with

Vaidya still asleep on the charpoy and reached the spot where his Lord Rama was holding Lakshman's hand, waiting.

The Vaidya jerked opened his eyes when Hanuman touched him slowly on his shoulder. Finding himself in a new place, the Vaidya was surprised and he was given the reason for his presence here. Since he was not to treat an enemy of his king Ravan, the Vaidya had a dilemma. Hanuman convinced him that as a medicine man he was supposed to help any human being. A medicine man's duty was to save a life no matter whose. Hanuman led him to the place where Lakshman lay unconscious and Rama sat still holding his brother's hand. A ripple of joy waved through the crowd at the arrival of a man who could take out the poison from Lakshman's body.

Vaidya took Lakshman's hands, and examined the injury and the type of poison he had gotten through the arrow. After he completed his examination he expressed his deep concern, "Can someone go and fetch Sanjivani from the Dronapuri Hills in Himalayan ranges? Only with this plant this poison can be removed. I'll need it before daylight."

This command from the Vaidya was something beyond apprehension. Kanyakumari at the southern end and the Himalayan range at northern part of Bharat, the name for India, was not a place one could reach and come back in such short time. Vaidya again repeated his command and verdict.

Hanuman as usual was the only one who came forward and offered his services for his Lord. Hanuman being a staunch devotee of Lord Rama, was always ready to do anything for his Lord. He left for the Himalayas, reciting Rama's name. He crossed over the ocean and the mainland of Bharat, flying swiftly toward the Himalayan range. Even though he encountered enemies on the way, he managed to reach his destination.

As instructed by Vaidya, he looked around but it was difficult to sort out which plant was Sanjivani. Each gave out *flashing lights at night time. He decided to pick up the whole hill so that the Vaidya could identify the plant.*

Hanuman reached the place where Lord Rama and all the others waited. They were surprised to see him coming back carrying the entire hill. Once he put the hill down, the Vaidya sorted out the Sanjivani plant himself. Lakshman regained consciousness after he was given the proper treatment by the Vaidya. Then Vaidya was taken back to his abode without any one's notice.

That was the story for that day. I was so drawn to the stories, that I continued attending till the end when Sita was rescued and they returned home on Diwali, the festival of light day, to Oyudha.

Without reading from any book, I learned the stories of Ramayana and Mahabharata from the storytellers of Manipur. Almost all the attendees were illiterate. Through these professional storytellers of Manipur, masses of the population in the valley of Imphal learned about the scriptures of the Holy Books of Ramayana and Mahabharata.

I am grateful to my beloved grandmother, Rajkumari Sanachaubi, who took me places so that I could learn the cultures and traditions of our society. The Mahabali temple still attracts lots of devotees, especially on Tuesdays. It is now motorable but still on the bank of the River Imphal and not too far away from the palace where the famous temple of Govindaji is situated. I hope you are aware of what it was like during those days, so different from the present. Now the children can only learn by reading the books of those stories. Bye for today.

Yours lovingly,
Ine

*   *   *

Journal Entry
Santa Cruz, California
August 19, 2006

The retreat by the Sri Sathya Baba organization.

At 8 am, I ride with Prasumna and Krishna Reddy after parking my car at their place. We are on our way to the monastery known as the Land of Medicine Buddha. We reach the place around 9:45 am. I get room #12 with Satya Karla. Morning bhajan after tea and snacks and Lunch between 1 and 2 pm. Study circle about Gita Vahini till 5 pm. After tea, we go hiking and back to the room by 7 pm. After dinner again study circle about Baba's teachings.

On 8/20 Satya Karla gives a presentation about her experience with Baba and about his teachings. She does Reiki too. Aroti, a Bengali lady, was an interesting figure. I didn't join morning Sankirtan but sat for meditation at the temple. We returned on the evening of the 20th even refreshed spiritually and physically.

Journal Entry
Toronto, Canada
December 1, 2006

Leaving for Toronto, Canada via Baltimore by red eye flight and reach Toronto early morning. On December 2, I can see the first snowflakes of the year covering all the green grass. Next day Lata, Louie and Bianca come over to pick me up. There was no snow at their place. But the third day snow starts falling as if it is following me. The next morning, Louie drops me at Eaton Center for me to go around and come

back with Lata by subway after her work. It is fun as I know
the area quite well.

*   *   *

San Ramon, California
April 20, 2001

Dear Gojen

*Itw was Sunday in the month of February 1950, I saw my
father, holding an invitation card in his hand and opening to
see whose invitation card it was. I could make out that it was
meant for a wedding. On the envelope it had my father's name
M Ibungohal Singh "and family."*

*According to our custom, unlike in the rest of India, the
caste is put before the name, though nowadays some are changing
the custom. I was curious to find out more and waited for my
father to hand the card over for me to read. In our house, only
my father and I were the ones who could read and write.*

*It was for the wedding of Thounaojam Babu Singh's
daughter. (Thounaojam is the surname and Babu Singh is the
first name.) When my father handed me the card, he casually
mentioned, "Do you know our yumnak/surname used to be
Thounaojam, not Maibam?"*

*That was a big surprise; nobody had told me that. My first
reaction was, "How did we become Maibam?"*

*"Well, this is how it was so far as I know." My father started
narrating the story about our ancestors and how the caste system
determined their lives. "My father Tomchou Singh, who was your
grandfather, was the son of Princess Chingoisana Devi, daughter
of King Nara Singh who ruled Manipur during 1844-1850."*

"When Chingoisana became of marriageable age the king, Nara Singha, started looking for a suitable match for his daughter. With the help of his advisors, he found Thounaojam Luwangba, a suitable groom for Chingoisana. But the King for some reason of his own wanted to change the surname to Maibam. As desired by the King, Luwangba and his family had to change their surname from their original Thounaojam to Maibam.

I listened with keen interest while my father narrated the story. Luwangba and Princess Chingoisana got married with the blessings from the King. They were blessed with three sons and a daughter. Ibungohal was the oldest, Iboyaima was the second and Tomchou was the third son. Tamphasana was the fourth and the only daughter.

When Tomchou was in his twenties he become an eligible bachelor, and he had many proposals for bride from good families. It was during the time of Janmashtami, a celebration of the Hindus for the birthday of Lord Krishna. He planned to go to the market Khwaramband Bazaar in downtown Imphal with his friends for shopping. To go to the market they had to cross Keishamthong Bridge and then after about one and half miles, they would be at Keishampat junction where roads from five different directions meet. The intersection led to different destinations of the town. My grandparent's house could be partially seen through the bamboo tree from the junction

This bridge was famous for people hanging out there. As traffic was unknown those days, people could just stand and spend their time chitchatting or just watching people passed by. Tomchou wanted to join some of his friends already hanging out there so he and his friends joined the group. Now and then a bicycle passed. Some people were going to the market to sell their products. Some were returning home.

During their conversations, Tomchou and his friends came to know about Lickol sannaba (game) happening that night at *the house of Keisham Koireng Singh. Lickol was some sort of a game played by the grown up girls during this season of August and September. They sat in a circle around a marked sheet on which six shells were used as dice. The person who got the maximum number of shells landing with the open face up was the winner. Young men from different localities were allowed to join the game and could sit next to a girl of their choice.*

That night the game was organized by the local girls of the Keisham Leikai at the house of Koireng Singh, who was a goldsmith and Royal jeweler. Leinou, the only daughter of Koireng Singh, was well-known for her beauty. Tomchou and his friend decided to come back and to join the game in the evening.

After confirming the location and time they proceeded toward market where they wanted to buy shirts for themselves, choosing from shopkeepers who were mostly from other states of India. That was good chance to wear a new one for the game.

After dinner and changing their clothes, they walked toward Keisham Leikai. When they arrived, the house was lit with a lantern and Patromax lamps. The game had already started and they saw few young men playing with the girls while others stood in front of the verandah watching the game and the girls.

There were six girls playing in a circle. They were in their best dresses known as Phanek (long stripped skirt), blouses, and Innaphi (scarf covering the upper body) and gold jewelry. The young men joining the game were mostly from different localities. Some sat beside the girls of their choice. Light from the Patromax lamps cast a warm glow around the front yard and the verandah. Tomchou and his friend also joined the few who stood watching the game. They could not join immediately until some of the young men got up to give them a turn. Tomchou for the first time saw Leinou and his attention was on her only. No doubt she was the prettiest. After about forty minutes, some of the men playing got up giving the ones standing and waiting a chance to play. Tomchau immediately took his place next to Leinau. His friend sat next to another girl. They all played the game, chattering and joking. Tomchou was too nervous to say more than a few words to the girl sitting next to him. Despite all he had planned to say, nothing was coming from his mouth; his feelings for her took control over him. He didn't want to leave his space but he had to, because others were also waiting to play the game. Leinau felt something special about this man but didn't know about him at all. Tomchou was determined to do something later on and left the game which was over by past midnight.

Tomchou did tell his friend about his feelings for this girl. "Be careful of the outcome," his friend warned. "Do you think your parents will agree to it?" His friends knew the girl is not from the higher caste as that of his friend Tomchou.

Tomchou made secret plans to approach someone he knew at Keishampat. After few days he came back to Keisham Leikai to see Yaima whom he had known for years. Occasionally they met at the Keishampat Bridge when he passed through on his way to the market.

It was sometime in the morning hours that he came to Yaima's house and saw him in the front yard looking at the vegetables growing in the kitchen garden. As Tomchou walked toward him, Yaima greeted him with a smile and a surprised look. He had never come to Yaima's house before. Moreover, they were not so close friends.

"Oh, welcome. What brings you here to my poor dwelling?" Yaima asked jokingly. He knew Tombhou belonged to a wealthy family of royal descendants.

"Friend, I need your help."

"What can I do for you?" Yaima didn't have a clue about his friend's intention.

"*I want you help me to convey a message to Leinou.*" He told Yaima very softly as if the air would spread the news. Tomchou was very serious about it.

Yaima instantly knew Tomchou's intention and he was not sure if he could help him. Because he was not so close to Leinau's family.

"*Sorry, I am not so close to Leinou's family but you can ask our neighbor Iche Thambal. She visits their home quite often and I can introduce you to her.*"

"*Please, I will be obliged to you forever.*" Tomchou was ready to do anything.

Thambal listened very carefully to what they wanted from her. When she came to know about Tomchou's background regarding his family, she realized it would not be an easy proposal. "*Come again next Wednesday. I shall let you know.*" Thambal didn't specify what she would do but kept his hope alive. Since there was some hope, Tomchou didn't insist more than was necessary and went back home with hope.

Thambal later on thought things over. Tomchou's parents would never agree to the proposal. The caste system was so much in vogue and surname Keisham was not going to be up to their liking. But if he was really in love with her there was no harm trying. They could overcome all the obstacles if they were truly in love. Thambal decided to try because she liked Leinou and wanted her to have a good husband.

The following week Thambal tried to find out more in detail about Tomchou from his neighborhood. She wanted to make sure that Leinou didn't involve with a wrong man. She knew immediately that Tomchou's mother, the princess Chingoisana would not welcome Leinau into her house as a bride. But Thambal knew that Tomchou was very serious and decided to help him.

Thambal came to Leinou's house a few days later and saw Leinau's mother Tampha busy cleaning and shining the gold *jewelry, which her husband had just finished making. Koireng, was a very busy goldsmith with group of helpers at his work station. That was the time he just completed making a Marai, a special gold necklace for the royal family, so his wife was helping polish the pieces. Thambal saw the busy schedule in the house and walked straight to Tampha.*

"Iche (elder sister), how are you doing? I am here to see a small chain for my future daughter-in-law."

Tampha looked up, "Thambal, so nice to see you after long time; when is the wedding?

"We have not fixed the date yet but It will be soon. She saw some gold chains. "I shall come back again after talking to my husband. Where is Leinou? I don't see her."

"She must be in the kitchen."

"I have not seen her for a long time, too. I shall go inside and see her."

Tampha just nodded to let her go in and resumed her work with the gold jewelry still working on it. Thambal walked toward the kitchen and saw Leinou in the kitchen cooking and Thambal grabbed a small stool lying nearby and sat on it, a bit away from the kitchen. Leinou welcomed her, surprised too to see Thambal as hey had not seen each other for some time now.

Thambal whispered, "Do you remember that boy in light blue shirt who sat next to you during Lickol?"

Leinau looked at Thambal in surprise and at the same time blushed a little.

"He is from Yaiskul and Maibam Family. He is the third son of Luwangba and Princess Chingoisana." There was some silence and after sometime she continued, "He is in love with you. He wants to meet you."

Leinau looked out in case her mother was around and heard their conversation. Still she didn't say a word, but she listened to Thambal.

"Next Wednesday he is coming to my house at three o'clock; he wants to meet you. Let me know what you think."

Leinou was hesitant to answer immediately. Again she looked toward her mother's direction. Then after some time Leinau said in a low voice, "Indon (Aunt) I shall try."

Thambal was pleased, "Remember he is coming around 3 pm next Wednesday. I have to send him a message of confirmation."

Thambal didn't waste any more time and got up to go while Leinau continued cooking the day's meal.

Since the day he had played Lickol, Tomchou was at the Keishampat Bridge hanging around with the other young men whenever he had the chance. When he got the message from Thambal he became more and more restless and anxious for the day of his visit to arrive.

Wednesday came after a long two-day wait for Tomchou.

On this day after finishing her daily chores at the house, Leinau asked if her mom needed anymore help. She said if not, she wanted to visit her friend Tombi in the neighborhood. Her mom looked at her lovingly and said, "Come back in time for the evening prayer (burning Dhup at Sanamahi, and outside near the door and also at the Tulsi plant in the middle of the front yard, a ritual for a Hindu Meitei family).

"Sure, Ima, I will be back in time."

It was nearly 3 pm. She quickly picked her innaphi (the scarf to wear on top of her skirt/phanek) and left her house. She walked as fast as possible in the direction of Thambal's house. Her friend Tombi's house was also at the same lane but two houses away from Thambal.

For the last 15 minutes Tomchou had been at Thambal's house looking toward the gate. He was as impatient as could be as time was ticking away and it was already past 3 pm. Now 3:10 pm. As Leinau entered the gate Tomchou quickly returned to the room where they were supposed to meet. Thambal welcomed her and asked her to come in and directed her toward the room where Tomchou was waiting for her. One mura was there near the door and a bit away from Tomchou. She took the stool and sat on it. Leinou kept quiet, her eyes on the floor. She didn't speak a word. After a long silence, Tomchou at last managed to say something.

"I don't know how you feel for me but I have been always thinking about you since the day we played the Lickol game. I can't forget you even for a minute."

She didn't answer but shifted her glance toward him and smiled. They both knew what was happening between them and were sure it was love.

He continued to say that he wanted her to be with him for the rest of his life. Still shy, Leinau couldn't answer anything directly but her eyes spoke just the same. As time clicked faster than expected, Leinau got up and said, "I have to go home. Ima will be expecting me now."

"Is it possible for us to meet same time next week?" he asked.

"I shall let you know later on." She didn't want to commit to anything as yet.

While Tomchou was watching her go through the window Thambal came in and asked, "How did it go?"

"Indon, I think she likes me, too."

"Please can you arrange? I want to see her again."

"I shall try," Thambal answered.

After a few months, Tomchou's parents came to know about their son's involvement with a Keisham girl. This was not acceptable to them. They even started talking to Tomchou about a girl of their choice for him. They already had chosen a girl of higher caste and from a wealthy family. Parents had the right to choose a girl or a boy for their children.

One evening when Tomchou came back home, he was immediately called to come in and to talk with his parents. He came in and stood in front of his parents without saying a word.

Princess Chingoisana started the conversation, "What we hear about you with the girl from Keishampat, I hope it is not true."

He didn't answer.

"We have a girl in mind for you; we have already talked and finalized with the parents. So stop seeing this girl." That was a command from the princess.

He didn't answer and went back to his bed and he was awake the whole night, turning from side to side. It was nearly six months or so he has been seeing this girl at Keishampat and now this order from his mother was something he didn't want to obey. The royal families and the society thought only about the caste system and nothing else. But he knew living without Leinau would be heartbreaking beyond his imagination. He also knew it was impossible to make his parents agree to his wishes. The senseless caste system was the barrier to the union of two hearts in love. "Whatever happens I am going to marry Leinau." So Tomchou decided not to listen to his mother.

Elopement was the solution. This remains a common practice in our society, though the caste system is no longer considered a factor. Education for boys and girls are the main factors in choosing brides and grooms in present day society.

When a girl was to elope with a boy she was usually kept in one of her friend's houses. The next morning, the message was conveyed to both their parents. The boys' relatives, with the help of the elders living in the locality, had to go to the girl's house to inform them about the elopement. If both sides agreed to the marriage, discussion followed about the details of the wedding. For Tomchau, it was not happening this way. His parents did not agree to accept the girl he loved into the family. He was told to leave the girl and come back home. He was not welcome at Yaiskul if he brought the girl with him.

Here the girl's side too was adamant. The men folk in the locality of Keisham Leikai gathered together and decided not to

*allow Tomchou to leave Keisham Leikai and go to his parents'
place. He was kept hostage in case his parents made him change
his mind. Leinau's parents were wealthy and she was their only
daughter. They could afford to arrange for a grand wedding
equal to that of a royal wedding.*

*Tomchou and Leinau got married in grand style at
Keishampat while none of Tomchou's relatives attended the
celebration. Tomchau had to sever relations with his family;
he and his wife lived at her parents' house. He was sad not to
be able, ever, to visit his ancestral home at Yaiskul. We are his
descendants. The plot of land we have at Keishampat is our
ancestral place.*

*My father narrated this story about our grandparents with
great enthusiasm and spirit. I could see my grandparents as a
young couple in love, how my grandfather's parents objected to
the marriage and disowned their son and his family. The events
ran through my mind as if they were depicted on a movie screen.
My grandfather's family were caught in the caste system. I felt
sorry for my grandfather and at the same time I admire him for
his true love of Leinau, my grandmother, the only woman in his
life.*

*From what I heard of my ancestors, I realized that the
Meities community I belong to was cocooned in the caste system.
Only after India became independent and the kingdom of
Manipur became a part of India in 1947/48 did the caste system
gradually lose its importance*

Yours lovingly,
Ine

* * *

Journal Entries
Trip to India
Poona
February 13, 2007

Since February 10, I am visiting India to see all my relatives there. I am at present with my sister-in-law Mohini and her daughter Shakun. We plan to go to Tirupati to see the famous South Indian Balaji Temple. Arranged by my niece, Shakun, a taxi takes us to Tirupati comfortably. After a night's stay at the Kalyani Residency Hotel near the railway station, we start for the Balaji Temple, which is on top of a hill at Tirumalai. The waiting line to get inside is about three hours even though we have special papers to go in. On the way back to Bangalore, we have lunch at Kamat Upahar, and the lunch is served on banana leaves as is the custom of the locality. February 12th is Bandh at Bangalore and hence we can't go out anywhere because of the Bandh. It is for demand of the Kauveri River for water distribution, more for Karnataka state. So we spend the day watching a Bollywood movie, "Jhankar."

February 13, 2007

We go to Bangalore's MG road. The old charm is no more. I am so disappointed. The lane we must take home to my niece's apartment is not paved and very bumpy. The rickshawala who gives us a ride comments that even dogs and cats do not like to come here. His remark amuses us, and we end up laughing even after he drops us.

*   *   *

Puttaparthy
February 14, 2007

Mohini and I left for Puttaparthy around 8:35 AM in a hired taxi to have darshan of Sri Satya Sai Baba. Puttaparthy, too, is no more like in the old times. The area has changed so much with new complexes that include a hospital, the Ashram, schools, colleges and airport, all built with marvelous architecture.

We arrive at Prasanthi Nilayam at 12 pm as our driver is a bit too careful while driving. After lunch we deposit our purses and bags and wait in the hall for Baba's darshan at 2:30 pm. Baba comes out around 4:20pm and he really looks so frail.

New Delhi
February 17, 2007

I come back to Delhi and stayed with my youngest sister-in-law Raj and her family in Jangpura, New Delhi. Next day Raj, Shalu and I go to my nephew Ravi's place in Raj's Maruti car. We find Ravi's wife Sonia is doing well as a teacher and Ravi is still struggling with his business. Arshi, their daughter is 14, in 9th grade, and their son, Anshu, is in fifth grade.

February 22, 2007

After visiting all my relatives on my husband's side, I now leave for Imphal where my brother Irabanta lives.

I see my brother keeps himself busy cooking. So much has changed after his wife passed away. His five-story building is built with architectural beauty and the healthy climbing up to the fifth floor keeps us exercising.

The next day, my cousin Mema takes me in her car to a nursery at Pahoi and later to Chorus Ratan Thyam's cultural center. That is something of a noteworthy place and the pride of Manipur.

February 25, 2007

We go to Moirang to visit Gojen's in-laws and we drive around to see Loktak Lake but somehow we miss the turn to Sendra and we come back home without seeing it.

The next day in the evening we go to Tera to meet Sonali, my half sister Sorojini's daughter. She is single with a son, as her husband who worked in police department was killed during an ambush. We took the phone number of her mother as I plan to visit Sorojini during our trip to Cachar for the wedding of our relative in Cachar.

March 3, 2007

The big festival of Yaoshang/holi starts today and people are in festive mood. Tomorrow, children will go around collecting money from houses just like I did as a young person, just like trick-or-treaters do during Halloween in the US. This occasion brings back the memories of my childhood days playing holi colors.

At Keishampat *Thabal Chongba* is going on with loud music to celebrate the festival of color. I can see the dances from the fifth floor of my brother's house.

* * *

San Ramon, California
May 17, 2001
Dear Gojen

As mentioned earlier, my brother Irabanta was just about five months old when we moved to Imphal and settled at Keishampat. My step-mother, Imashi Tamphasana was still young and a lively woman. When Irabanta was about two years old, she bore a second son. At this time, my father's involvement with yet another woman stirred up unpleasant feelings in the family. When at about two years of age, the second son became ill with dysentery and passed away from this ailment that could have been cured easily but wasn't. My grandmother blamed my father for spending so much time with another women rather than taking care of his son. So my Grandmother used her same strategy again suggesting my father bring his new love to live with us at the house. He readily agreed and brought Thabal from Thangmeiband to join our family.

Figure 11
R K Tamphasana

We were six now, my father, mother, Imashi Tamphasana, Irabanta, my grandmother and myself. Even with a full house, we managed to give father's latest addition a room. My father's income was just enough for for us to lead a comfortable life, and we didn't have to worry about food, clothing and shelter. Thabal must have gotten the impression that Father was a very wealthy man and so fell for him. This time, we didn't have to seek out a

magic wand. Living with us, she realized that there was not much of a future, and she left after only few months. My mother was used to this way of living with my father and she didn't seem to bother much now.

After Thabal left, Imashi Tamphasana became pregnant for the third time. My mother was busy quietly doing her usual household chores. I never heard her utter a negative word. Sometimes I heard verbal fights between my father, grandmother, and Tamphasana but

Figure 12 Grandmothre with my brothers

never my mother. She was busy looking after my brother Irabanta and me when another baby boy was delivered on November 23, 1951. He was named Tuleswer. Irabanta had always been under the care of my grandmother and by now he was five years old.

I had just finished my final examination in April of 1952. In May a tragedy struck in our family. Imashi Tamphasana became sick and in the beginning she didn't take it seriously thinking the problem was ordinary diarrhea, but it turned out to be serious and frightening. I remember the commotion in the

Figure 13 Mother with my brothers

house and everyone looking worried. Someone was sent for the Maiba (local medicine man), and my father had gone to call a doctor. The medicine man was available immediately, but the doctor took some time to arrive, as he had gone to see another patient. I watched Imashi Tamphasana in the front room with the Maiba. He was instructing her to try to urinate but she couldn't, only watery stool draining her body away because of the infection of cholera germs. She had probably gotten the cholera germ in her system after eating singju (salad) sold in the local store. The herbal medicine given by the medicine man didn't work. Tamphasana became pale and weak and seemed to realize that the end of her life was approaching. I could see in her eyes that the fearof death and worried about her few months old baby.

My mother stood near her giving her assurance that she would be alright but it was understood what was coming. She looked at my mother anxiously and with a low whimper, "The baby is under your care." My mother still held her hand giving a slightly tighter grasp, tears rolling down. After those few words, Tamphasana lost her consciousness. My father came back with the doctor only to find her lifeless body. I could see the remorse in my father's eyes, but there was nothing he could have done. The cholera germs multiplied too quickly in her blood stream causing her body's collapse so soon.

My seven—month-old baby brother was now under the care of my mother. She took special care that the baby was fed properly. Now he depended only on a milk bottle. That was how both the boys grew up under the care of my grandmother and my mother.

Your dad Irabanta was five years old when his birth mother passed away, but he does not remember anything. I am sure you now know how the tragedy happened and how both your dad

Irabanta and your uncle Tuleswer grew up under the care of grandmother and mother.

Yours lovingly,
Ine

*   *   *

Journal Entry
Imphal, India
March 7, 2007

Irabanta and I leave for Guwahati for the wedding of Imashi Tamphasana's sister's grandson who lives in Cachar. Mr. and Mrs. Hazarika are in the airport to receive us. I stay with the Hazarikas while Irabanta goes to Hotel Evergreen where the wedding party is. The bride who is a non Manipuri is from Guwahati and hence the wedding ceremony is to be held here.

*   *   *

San Ramon, California
June 29, 2001

Dear Gojen

April 2, 1952 was the most important day of my life as my matriculation exam was scheduled on this day. This examination was regularly held under the University of Guwahati after one completed the 10th grade, and it was a gateway to our future professions depending on how well we did in our chosen subjects. Only nine of us from Tamphasana Girls' High School took the examinations. Previous batches of girl students had been even smaller than ours. Today is the first day of the exam on English literature. I kept revising Shakespeare's dialogue looking at the pages of the book. It was so different the way we were taught in the class from the present day system. I still wonder how we learned that way. I was ready to leave for the examination while my grandmother and mother said a prayer for me. Just as I took my steps toward our main door, I saw someone approach our gate. It was my cousin brother Haricharan from Yaiskul! He hardly visited our house, but this day he came in to give me moral support. What a pleasant surprise. He was on his way to his office and wanted to accompany me up to the school. I was thrilled to have someone to give me moral support.

"Are you ready for the exam? He asked.

"I am so nervous Tamo/ Elder brother"

"Just try to relax. Everything will be okay."

"Thank you. Tamo, I shall try."

We walked together along the road toward our school, which was about 15 minutes away. On the way, I was peeping at pages of my book.

"You don't need to look into the book now; whatever you have learned, it is already in you."

"I am feeling so nervous still," I responded.

We reached school and my cousin bid me goodbye, wishing me best of luck. I thanked him and turned toward the examination hall. I saw some of my friends were already there and I looked for my assigned seat. I was in the front row. More friends arrived and took their seats.

This incident is forever a memory inscribed deep in my heart and soul. My cousin, who has left now for his eternal abode leaving behind a wife and four children, showed me how happiness can be given to someone by doing little things. My cousin was a caring and loving person.

Not only was the year 1952 the gateway to my future, it was also important because of historical events. In April President Truman seized steel mills to prevent a strike. In July, Eisenhower was nominated as Republican presidential candidate in USA.

After about two and half months, the results of the matriculation examination were out. There was tension among the youth hanging around all over Imphal town waiting for the results to be posted. Most of the boys went to the center where results would be posted on the bill board on a wall. Around 8 pm, someone gave me the happy news

Figure 14 My cousin M. Haricharan Singh

that I had passed in the second division. We had a system known as first, second and third divisions. My other friend who lived in the neighborhood also got through and I was the only one who got second division. The only one who passed in the first division was Maipakpi. Oh, I was so thrilled and so excited. I felt like a hero in our locality as getting second division was something commendable for humanities/arts subjects. I saw the happiness and pride in my father as he heard the news.

Now that I had to join college my problem was transportation there. Where I had earned admission in Arts and Humanities required walking or biking. But I didn't have a bike and hence never learned how to bike. Remember, having a bike was as important then as having a car is to us now. My father got me a bicycle so that I could ride to the college even though we had never before had extra money for buying me a bike. Now I had to learn fast so that I could ride to college in August. I had a very tough time learning at age 16. I used to come out to the main road early in the morning so that no one was around to see me fall down again and again. Hurting my back and buttocks, also my head, I continued my trial and error learning. One fine, morning I woke up from a dream that I was biking all over the locality. It felt so real that I couldn't brush off the good feeling for some time. But reality struck when I took out my bike again on the road. Within a couple weeks, though, I graduated to the status of cyclist. I could ride without falling. I felt as if I was walking on the moon.

At the college campus, we girls were only five among hundreds of boys. It was a big change for us as up till now we had always been in separate schools from boys. We were lucky girls because in those days girls were not usually encouraged by their parents to pursue higher education. Damayanti, one of my good friends who lived near our area, was one of the lucky ones. The most admirable girl among us was Maipakpi, who had to attend college by walking five miles from home, back and forth. People couldn't help but admire her. Joymati from Yaiskul, daughter of Dr. Bhaigo, became one of my closest friends in my college days in Imphal.

A few weeks after the college session started, elections were coming up for the students' union. I was asked to stand for it from a group belonging to the Socialist party. I didn't know anything about the politics. Neither had I known about the campaign we had to do for getting more votes. I responded, "I don't know anything about it."

"Don't worry, we will do everything."

Figure 15 D M College Social Service Corp 1953

"Then, it is okay; you can put my name out." I responded without any intention of learning or trying for the votes from the students.

The Socialist party chose me as a candidate for secretary of the music and entertainment committee. The boy who stood opposite me had a very lovable nature and could sing local and Hindi film songs very well. I never ventured to ask anyone for a vote. How stupid I was. Even though I knew nothing about the role of the secretary, I still went ahead with the election. That boy won with an overwhelming number of votes. I think he really deserved it. Unfortunately this young and charming man committed suicide after some months because of personal problems in his life. It was a very sad for his family.

There were other elections for posts of secretaries for sports, social services volunteer work and more, but the main candidate was for the general secretary of the students' union.

My friend Joymati and I volunteered for the social services (sitting in the front row in the picture) of the association of Social Service Corp of DM College.

(My friend Joymati and I were the only ones among the girls who participated in the social service program.)

The old Koirengei airport, built during WWII during the fighting with Japan was near our college. My first year of college was full of hope and fun because for the first time we were able to go around independently. Joymati and I used to go the airport to see how the planes landed. Both of us had never been in an airplane nor had we seen any planes landing. Planes had come to the Imphal airport once a week. Those people who wanted to fly were in long lines and many were waiting lists. Nowadays three or four flights land in Imphal daily. So I just want you know how things were during my time there.

During the time plane landed, we stood watching with the hope of seeing air hostesses, who were very pretty ones. None ever came out. Once the passengers deplaned and the luggage was taken out from the plane, the luggage of waiting passengers was loaded inside the aircraft, and those waiting were called to proceed to the aircraft. We stood with the passengers until they started boarding. There were no restrictions for visitors in those days.

Another of our favorite places to visit was the cemetery of WWII soldiers who gave their lives for their countries. We felt sad when we read the names of the young soldiers from Allied forces from different countries. Some were only 16 to 18 years of age and never got the chance to reach maturity and manhood. Since we did not hang out with the boys, these excursions were the way we girls entertained ourselves.

Another memorable day during my college days was a UN day celebration. Our college organized a short skit to be performed in Rupmahal Theater. I was asked to play the role of Vijaya Lakshmi Pandit, who was Nehru's sister. Pundit Jawaharlal Nehru was the first Prime Minister of India after the country's Independence from the British on August 15, 1947. He had served the country till May 27, 1964, when he died in office. Vijaya Lakshmi Pandit was at that time an envoy to the UN from India. She led an Indian delegation to the UN from 1946 to 1948 and again from 1952-1953. I was proud of playing a revered world figure, especially one who was an Indian woman. Born on the 18th of August 1900, she served her country till she passed away on December 1st 1990. I didn't have many lines in my role as Indian envoy in the UN Observation Day play. As Vijayalakshmi Pandit, I was only to tap the bell on the table signaling that the time for a member's speech was up. My father was in the audience at the theater and after the play, we walked back home together. When we reached home he proudly informed my mother and grandmother that people were asking about me and about whose daughter I was. Even though he did not say anything else, I knew he was quite proud of me.

*The years 1952 to 1954 at DM College were my last years
with students from Imphal. The first year passed by very quickly
and in the second year, we didn't do much except study for our
next exam, the Intermediate, which was coming up.*

*But I did join the women's hockey team. We practiced at
Nagamapal Lairembi Lumpak. Other players included Bamon
Jamuna from Wahengbam Leikai and Momon from Nagamapal.
When the results were out for the Intermediate examinations, I
found I had gotten the highest score among the girls, passing on to
second division and receiving a scholarship. But things changed
and I had to go to another direction of my life.*

*The head clerk of the civil hospital came to our house
unannounced. He wanted to inform me that there was a good
course in Delhi for me. The Indian government had introduced
a degree in nursing at Delhi University and the college was
admitting women students from all of the Indian states.
The Manipur Government had just gotten the letter seeking
prospective candidates.*

*My mother went inside to make tea and I stayed there
listening to the clerk talk about the course in nursing, which I
had no interest in joining. My grandmother and father listened
quietly as he told us about what he believed was a very good
opportunity for me.*

*I did think the scholarship for me to attend at Delhi
was attractive as I longed to go and see the world and Delhi,
the capital of India, would be a good start. Although I wasn't
interested in nursing, I opted for the scholarship. For now, he
told us, arts and humanities students accepted for the second
division would be allowed into the all-science school as long as
they took the provided short basic course in physics, chemistry,
and biology.*

*My grandmother asked for more details. "After passing the
course, what will be her prospects?"*

"*I am sure she can go further to do a medical line. It is a new Government of India program and only two students are selected from each state,*" *he answered. No one knew the ultimate answer.*

The head clerk came again the next day and explained more about the course and convinced my parents that it was a good chance for me. We had to take examinations in English and Hindi. My father took the paper and told the clerk to give us some more time to think things over. My mother kept quiet.

Within two days it was decided that I would be going to Delhi for this course of study and we would have to make all the arrangements soon. My mother's cousin brother was ready to escort me to Delhi. I am so grateful to that uncle for always helping us. Finally I was to join Rajkumari Amrit Kaur College of Nursing, New Delhi. The session was to start sometime in August, 1954.

We came to know there were a few Manipuri students who would be studying in Delhi and made plans for me to leave Imphal on the same flight as they and to go with them to Delhi by train from Calcutta. My first journey by airplane! I had only gone to the airport before to see the planes landing and taking off. On the first flight, I felt quite nauseated and promised myself not to go again by air.

While in Calcutta, I went to meet Arambam Soroj Nalini, a girl senior student from Manipur and studying there. We were very happy to see each other. Suddenly she pointed at me. "Jamuna, you're wearing the sari wrong." She showed me how to tuck the pleats the other way than I had. Our dress was again different from the rest of India. Thank God she pointed this out to me before I reached Delhi. I would have been very embarrassed. My uncle took guidance from fellow travelers and students, and we worked out taking the train from Howrah station at Calcutta/Kalikota to the New Delhi Station.

Once there, my uncle took me straight to the college hostel, a vacant military barrack now used as hostel for the college, located at 12 Jaswant Singh Road. Staff and students of the college were accommodated together at this barrack. (It was a few years after my graduation that the college inaugurated a new College Campus with hostel at Lajpat Nagar 4 New Delhi 110024.)

My uncle and the student who accompanied me to the hostel found my room quite big for two girls to share. Dipti Sen was my roommate. She was back to repeat the year. I felt lucky to meet girls from all over India as our class was the largest yet, thirty women students, most sent by their state governments and some funded by their parents

Beginning in August, college classes were held in another vacant military barrack. We started with lectures and demonstrations by Miss Buchanan in nursing theory and art. She was from Canada, and I was lost for nearly a month as I found it hard to understand her pronunciation.

As part of our coursework, we were taken to the hospital by bus early mornings for practical training. Our uniform was a white sari and white blouse with a sleeveless white jacket. We didn't have to wear a cap until our second year.

Figure 16 Queen Suraiya, RKAmrit Kaur, Miss Craig, Principal.

Foreign dignitaries, usually female, were invited to visit our college. One was the visit of Queen Saroiya of Iran who was considered the most beautiful woman in the world at that time. For a special program to entertain VIPs, a few girls were chosen to learn dances from a Bengali teacher at the college. I was one of them. We performed Bengali folk dances to entertain the visiting VIPs, Rajkumari Amritkaur, then Minister of Health and Medical Services among them.

The final exam came around fast and I got through all the subjects except the science subjects. Since I didn't get through, these science subjects in my first year, I took the test in my second year and I passed!

Our second year milestone was our capping ceremony. The ceremony and our caps helped us honor the noble profession we had entered to serve others in need.

During our second year of school, Lady Mountbatten of Burma visited. We were introduced to her and entertained her with a big welcome tea party on our barrack lawn.

Dipti Sen shared the hostel room with me till our final year. Even though we were roommates, we were not close as friends. Deokala from Kalimpong near Darjeeling was my best friend. We confided in each other about our personal lives. We were very fond of having our pictures taken at a shop in Janpath, then Queensway. The shop was owned by two fellows, both deaf and mute. They did a good job in their profession; we were always satisfied with the results. My other good friends were Arati Dowerah and Sabita Bhunya from Assam, our neighboring state. Shayesta was another girl from Assam, who became a good friend till the end of our college days. Roma Roy, Bani Ghosh, Manju Basu and Reena Ghosh were from Bengal and we used to hang out together. I had many other friends, both from Bengal and from other states. Krishna Bhatia, Uma Herabet from Mumbai, Sheethalaxmi from Madras, Satwant kaur and Beat Kaur from Punjab.

Our hostel food was calculated by our nutritionist as a balanced diet. But we never liked the food. Bengali girls were quite fond of seafood. One day a few of us went to India Gate where artificial lakes were filled with fish. We took a thin cloth to use as our net and swept it around bunches of swimming fish.

Surprisingly we caught a lot and we planned to fry them in our room. Roma Roy was using a new electric stove for cooking and we all sat watching her fry the fish. When the cooking was nearly finished and we were ready to eat it

Figure 17 Hand shake with Lady Mountbatten of Burma

with rice already cooked, we heard footsteps and a knock on the door. The warden's room was quite far away from ours and there was very little chance she would have known what we were doing. But the smell of fried fish reached some of the other girls' rooms and they reported it to the warden.

"Who is it?" one of us asked.

"Warden" By now the smell of fried fish must have reached her nose. "Open the door."

"One minute." We quickly we put an old electric stove that was lying nearby on top of the hot electric stove we were using. The old stove was warm enough to make her believe we'd been using it and had just finished.

"One minute." We took time as much as we could, then as the door opened the smell of the fried fish rushed out.

"You know you cannot cook inside the hostel?" Our warden thundered.

"Sorry we won't do again."

We handed her the old one which was warm enough. We're happy that she hadn't bothered to come inside to check but she was satisfied and left with the old stove instead.

"This is the last warning, your off days will be cancelled for the week if you do it again"

"Yes, Ma'am" we understand."

After she left, we ate our share of the meal; it was the tastiest food we'd had at school all term.

I used to get pocket money of 20 rupees per month from home, and that was a big amount. I could do so many things: go for a movie and shop at Janpath and stop for food. We had a short cut to Janpath/Queensway from our college. Our favorite place was Madras hotel for dosa and dal barra.

In our second year, we were sent to the village Chawla for six weeks for experience as rural public health nurses. The cook there prepared home-cooked food unlike our college hostel food. We made home visits by bike during the area's summer heat. We carried wet towels to cover ourselves under that burning sun and heat. We believed if we could survive that training we could survive anywhere.

We used puppets in demonstrations and lectured the village women and children on how to take care of their health and hygiene. In spite of my own lean and thin figure, I had fallen sick only once, suffering a high fever and staying in the infirmary. It turned out to be malaria and I was treated accordingly. Our principal Miss Craig came to see me and said, "You must put on 10 lbs. within two months." I ate whatever I got but I never gained weight and remained as it was till I got married and had my first baby in 1962.

My fourth year brought more responsibility because we were caring for rural and urban pregnant mothers before and during child birth. We had night duties and also rushed to homes whenever we were called. I still remember how we had to deal with difficult patients. Some of them welcomed us and some were just unfriendly.

Every year end we had a one-month vacation. Myself from Manipur and three girls from Assam couldn't afford to travel by air, so we took train from Delhi to Assam changing three times because there was no train going straight to Assam. And there was no Bramhaputra Bridge so we had to cross the gigantic Bramhaputra River by ferry. Aroti and Shaista were from Dibrugarh and Sabita was from Lower Assam; hence, she was home before crossing the river. At Dimapur, I had to switch to a bus to Imphal. Arati and Shaiyata had to go farther to Dibrugarh. Nowadays there is a direct train and the bridge over the Brahmaputra River makes it much easier to cross. When we travelled we bought tickets for third class compartments for ladies only, and tried to settle ourselves comfortably even though we did not have any seating reservations. It was quite an experience for us and we became smarter every year when we travelled, acting as if we all had upper class ticket, which we couldn't afford. May be the inspector pitied on us as he knew we were students. To use the common rest room, one had to have upper class ticket which we couldn't afford. When we managed to use the common rest room he didn't bother us.

I graduated in 1958 and returned home with my suitcases; my father came to receive me at Dimapur taking the public transport bus. My bicycle was booked to be shipped to my home address, and I got it after about a month. A job was still to be created especially for me in the medical department.

That year of my graduation, July 1958, Alaska became the 49th state of the USA while Hawaii became 50th State the following year. While I waited for the job, I got calls for home visits for delivery of babies. I earned quite a good income from that. But sometimes in the middle of the night getting a call, I was very upset as I wanted to sleep. But to keep the clients happy

I had to sacrifice my sleep most of the time. I reminded myself that I was in this profession to help and serve other people.

Yours Lovingly,
Ine

*   *   *

Journal Entries
San Ramon, California
April 3, 2007

I miss my friends in Valencia in Southern California. As we used to meditate together regularly we became very close. After I moved to Northern California, I became involved with my work at the JCPenney salon and meditating with others was no longer possible. At a time when many people start thinking of retiring, I am trying to start a new career. But one thing is significant about this profession—one can work as long as one wishes, there is no scarcity of jobs, and one can also decide the hours.

April 15, 2007

I just finished reading Amulya Malladi's novel *Mango Season*, about a girl named Priya a Telegu who lives in the US and visits her family in Hyderabad. Very well written and presented.

April 26, 2007

I attend the book launch for Linda Joy Myers' *Becoming Whole: Writing Your Healing Story* in Corte Madero, CA. Seven ladies, whose work appears in the book read, too. Lily gives me a ride with her husband, who accompanies her to the launch. We have lunch at the restaurant.

Journal Entry
June 1, 2007

Pangila and I join a Princess cruise to the Hawaiian Islands. It is one week of cruising around the islands. One night during the cruise I wake up and afraid we are missing the tour to Lahaina.

We do some shopping at Maui. We take a tour on a local bus and walk around, seeing the second largest tree in the world, the banyan tree is something unforgettable.

*   *   *

San Ramon, California
September 10, 2001
Dear Gojen

After I graduated in 1958 my new situation was dim. I did not get a job immediately and I had to wait for it to happen. There was a long process to go through the system, and I impatiently waited. During that time I was trying to contact the officers who could proceed with my papers officially so that my job could be created. As I wrote before, at this time I was having lots of house calls for the delivery of babies. I no doubt didn't want to get up in the middle of the night whenever the calls came but I had to.

My father on the other hand started blaming my grandmother and me for taking up this profession as there was no job. Well, I wished he would give at least some moral support. After all, he had been for this course of study when the choice was made. But as I think of it now, that was his nature.

The medical officer in charge of the Civil Hospital went all out to help me, but as with all government procedures, it moved at a snail's pace. So much time was wasted in processing at the main administrative office. I had to go and contact so many officers for the continued processing my application. The government of Manipur had sent me for the course but they were still not ready to give me job.

After about five months, I at last got the job as a sister in charge of the surgical ward in the Civil Hospital. The monthly pay started at Rs 250, which was a big sum of money in those days. I wore the same uniform I had from the College of Nursing, the white sari and the cap of the college. But wearing a white sari was not a good thing for an unmarried girl according to the medical officer who happened to be a Bengali. So I changed into the one the hospital had that time.

Well, I had good relationships with my co-workers, who were compounders, nurses, ward attendants and also our doctors in charge like Dr. Kala Singh and Dr. Kuladhaja Singh. I was asked to give classes for the student nurses on the subject nutrition. Later, I was also in charge of a nursing students' hostel, and I stayed with the students for some time until I got married.

After working there for about three years, I learned through the medical office that a scholarship was to be given for attending a program for advanced studies in nursing in

Australia. I received a letter for an interview on April 6th 1961. I was thrilled at the prospect of going abroad to pursue further studies.

Here is one thing I have not mentioned so far in my letters. The first love letter I received from a boy had only three sentences. That was when I had just taken my matriculation examination. I immediately fell in love with the letter and ultimately with the writer. But destiny played its part, and I feel everything happened for a reason. So our relationship mostly through letters ended when I had just finished my nursing studies. Even though I was happy that I worked and contributed to helping my parents, my emotional life was going down the drain. I could not relate to anyone who could help me. I had some moral support from close friends but nothing really gave me hope. My heart was broken and the pain persisted. My healing and my destiny began with the call from Delhi that I was wanted for an interview regarding the studies in Australia.

Yours lovingly,
Ine

*   *   *

Journal Entries
San Ramon, California
January 21, 2008

Met Mary Hogarty for lunch at the Bub's restaurant, Las Positas and talked about our work schedule. I am to be a co-coordinator of Fore Women Golf Association's egg group. I had planned to write my poetry and articles in my own convenient time. Started playing golf regularly at the same time. Shobha also gave $5000.00 for my expenses for the year. I don't know how my life would be without her.

February 18, 2008

I prepare my decorative salad and get camera ready with all the accessories for the lunch party at Mary Hogarty's place. GPS didn't give me proper guidance and, without a back up directions from the Internet, I drive up Morgan Hill for an hour. I come back home without going to the lunch, exhausted mentally and physically.

June 15, 2008

I write an article titled "Love and Hate Relationship with My GPS" and it is published on the Triond website. This is the first time I've published an article since I finished high school. I started golfing with the EGG of FWGA regularly and I love it.

"Golf is like a love affair. If you don't take it too seriously, it is no fun; if you take it seriously, it breaks your heart. (Actor Arnold Daly)

A poem on my golfing experience:

My Ball Lies There

Behind the ball I stand,
Favorite club in my hand,
A glorious shot I give
With a wish for the ball
To land near the hole.

I am stunned,
Watching it fly nowhere near the aim.
Darting off, it lands in water.
"Oh, my friend, why drown me?"
I hear its anguish cry.
My heart quivers to watch
The ball at the bottom
And clear water above.
Being beyond my power to retrieve it
The abandoned ball now rests there
Waiting for a savior to come
While I am being swept by waves of guilt.
But hope and dream being part of life
I pursue my game, wonderful shots
Still intact in my wishful thinking,
The act of playing golf continues
While my ball lies there.

October 5, 2008

I'm at my friend Pangila's place, where I have come to wish her a happy birthday. Pangila's son, Rupinder, takes us to the Peacock Restaurant in Santa Clara. I stay the night at her place and return home the next day after lunch.

*　　*　　*

San Ramon, California
August 20, 2002

Dear Gojen,

That was the time I was deep down in my emotional turmoil. When youth's prime time is severed with frustration and disappointment, one can become suicidal. If one can come out of it unharmed, the scar is left on the heart.

> "But there is something beautiful
> About all scars
> Whatever nature.
> A scar means the hurt is over,
> The wound is closed
> And healed, done with."
> (author unknown)

Something happened that April 2, when I was on my way to the Imphal airport to reach Delhi for the interview for post-graduate studies in nursing. My very good friend Saroj accompanied me to the airport. She was one of my closest friends; we confided in each other about our lives. We were in a hired jeep. As we reached the airport much ahead of time, after checking in my luggage, we sat down in empty chairs next to one another. There were other passengers already waiting in the lounge. We looked around to see if anyone we knew was traveling on the same flight. There was no one we knew. We just sat chatting about our activities while waiting for the aircraft to arrive. There was an announcement that it was still in Calcutta for some mechanical problem and would be delayed by another 25 minutes.

Saroj looked around. "Jamuna, look at that fellow in the brown striped shirt; he has the latest Filmfare *magazine in his hand."*

"Should I ask him to lend it to us if he is finished reading it?" I responded.

"Sure, we have plenty of time, after we look at it, we can give him back before the plane boards."

So I got up and played the bold girl in approaching a Mayang (name for the non—Manipuri from other states of India) man.

I walked slowly toward the gentleman. "Can I borrow your Filmfare *for few minutes?"*

"Sure." He looked quite surprised and at the same time happy to lend it to us. He handed me the magazine, and I walked back to my seat and gave it to Saroj to read. We were both crazy for the popular magazine's stories about movie celebrities. We looked at the pictures of the movie stars and read their stories without skipping any page. When the aircraft landed and we were preparing to board, I gave the magazine back to the gentleman with thanks.

After the announcement to board, we got up and I headed toward the aircraft while Saroj stood watching me. Just before entering the plane, I looked back and saw her turning toward the vehicle she had to ride back. Once inside the aircraft I settled myself at my assigned seat by a window. Two seats were still to be occupied.

Most of the passengers were seated when I saw the gentleman who had lent us the magazine coming toward my side. His seat was next to mine. I was surprised. Was it a just coincidence or he had changed the seat with someone else, I wondered. He settled himself in his seat. After some time he introduced himself. "I am Rup." I didn't tell him my name and just smiled and kept quiet. Then he asked me where I was heading. I was hesitant to tell him but thought he was nice to lend us his magazine and so I told him about the interview.

"Oh, my family lives in Delhi."

Both of us kept quiet for some time. I presumed he was also on his way to Delhi to see his family.

"My interview is on the 6th of this month. I have to be in Delhi before that."

Then he mentioned Mr.K, who was his friend.

"I know him very well; he comes to our hospital very often for his supply of surgical goods." I was taken aback with surprise. Mr.K had never mentioned his friend and neither had I seen him with Rup. And so I was doubtful that Rup knew Mr.K well.

"He talks a lot about you; he is in love with you."

I had heard this from a family friend, who was a prominent surgeon. He had said that Mr.K had been talking about me.

"He is very serious."

"He must be an ever romantic fellow." I was amused.

Rup was silent for some time. "Are you going to visit your family?" I asked.

He didn't answer immediately, smiled and said, "Yes, to see my family."

"Your wife and kids?" I presumed that he was a married man as he looked quite old enough to have wife and kids. He was overweight and looked to be in his mid-thirties.

"No I am not married yet." Then he told me about his parents and siblings living in Patel Nagar, New Delhi.

Then I told him Mr.K was just one of the medical representatives who came to the medical office to sell pharmaceutical products and surgical instruments. He sold surgical instruments and that was the reason to come to the surgical ward to meet the doctors in charge. My friendliness may have made him misunderstand my intentions.

After we reached Calcutta we had to purchase our train ticket to Delhi. Rup offered to buy mine and I accepted his offer. After he got the tickets, we took the Kalka Maill train. It took 24 hours, but I could not afford an air ticket to Delhi. I paid him back the amount. Rup took the money but later he expressed that he was surprised I had given him back the cost of the train fare. He thought girls usually took advantage of men. I was quite different, he said. Well, I was flattered. Slowly, I started trusting him as we travelled in the same compartment and he talked all about his family.

I felt I could confide in him and I started telling him about my life, about being heartbroken as my first love broke up with me and hence I was now planning to go away to Australia. He was surprised to hear that as all he knew about me was that Mr.K was in love with me.

He talked to me as true friend as we journeyed together up to Delhi. We got to know each other a bit. When we reached Delhi the next day, I headed for the Member of Parliament's quarter and he left for his home at South Patel Nagar New Delhi. As I had free time before the interview, he wanted to return and take me out to Queensway now Jan Path where people usually go for shopping.

He came on his brother-in-law's motor bike and took me where I had to meet one person before the interview, and then we went around Queensway and Connaught Place for shopping.

One day after the interview, he invited me to his older sister Dhuru's house for lunch. His parents were out of town, and hence his youngest sister Rajkumari came for the lunch, too. She was in 7th standard and looked very cute. My instant impression of his family was they were decent. According his family, the complexion of a girl was their main criterion for marriage. Later his sister Raj told me that she had put her palm near my face to *compare my complexions. Well, it looked like I was within the range of fairness they usually accepted.*

I started having strong feelings for Rup and he must have felt the same, because I came to know that he was actually going to Mumbai for his cousin sister's wedding but had changed his mind and decided to go to New Delhi with me.

We came back to Imphal via Lucknow as we could save money and spend some time together. That was the beginning of our emotional involvement and I realized I was in love, which I thought would never happen again. After we came back to my home town, Rup and I met quite often but I waited for some time to tell my parents because I was not sure what their reaction would be. Eventually, Rup and I knew we could not live without each other. As usual someone leaked the news to my parents about our affair and my father immediately informed my grandmother.

"Your father was informed of your involvement with a Mayang." I knew one day they would have to be told about it.

"Yes, I was planning to tell you we want to get married."

In those days, a Manipuri Meitei girl marrying an outsider was something unthinkable. Even though quite a few had already married outsiders, it was not an acceptable proposal in our society. My parents were worried about how to proceed with the plan. I knew they would not have the courage to announce and arrange this marriage. Ultimately, Rup and I decided to go to Calcutta and get married there.

Rup arranged through a friend who worked in the airline office for our marriage in a court in Calcutta. That was the time my cousin Purnimashi was with us and she was to be dropped at her mother's house in Lakhipur, Cachar. It was a coincidence that I had to go to Silchar for escorting my cousin and then I could proceed to Calcutta. So I took leave from my work and flew to Silchar with cousin Purnimashi.

As soon as we got out of the plane, she said, "I left my packet on the seat." She rushed back while I stood wondering what was in her packet. We took a bus to Lakhipur from Silchar and I stayed one night at Aunt Pashot's place. As usual my aunt always cried when I left. That was the last time I saw her and I still feel sorry wondering why I didn't visit her again. Rup's friend was from Utter Pradesh, a state in Northern India and married a Bengali widow at the same court in Calcutta. So he knew the procedure and everything was ready for us to proceed with the court wedding.

When I reached Calcutta from Silchar, Rup was waiting for me at the airport. As everything was already arranged and we went to the court straight. My friend from the College of Nursing, Reena Ghosh, was at that time in Calcutta and she was one of my witnesses. The judge married us and signed the court papers. In the evening, our witness and we headed to Lake, a tourist spot, in a taxi accompanied by one of Rup's friends. That ended in a minor mishap as the driver hit something jolting those of us in the passenger seats. Our guest had a minor cut in his forehead and we decided to turn back and go to our hotel.

The next day, we took a flight to Bagdogra and headed for Darjeeling. During the bus ride, I lost my broach, which was a gift from a pen friend in England. I had a sentimental attachment to it and I was sad for sometime. Rup was just struggling with his business and he didn't have extra money for a luxurious honeymoon. He had to ask his mom to send some money. Anyway, we were happy.

Drowning in the well of sorrow
Tangled with the broken hopes
Reckless tears in stream like a broken dam
Without a hope of coming out of it

I resigned myself to my fate.
The stars pitied on me and sent an angel
To save a fallen soul.

We came back to Imphal after our honeymoon in Darjeeling and announced our marriage. The uproar from people and relatives and friends was something I could never forget. My mother's cousin and our neighbor who worked for the secret service joined together and insisted

Figure 18 Our first house, Imphal

that I should be separated from Rup immediately. I wonder why they were so much against it while my own parents took it calmly, though they didn't show that to the public.

We survived. We gave a reception party through one of our friends who acted as a host. Those who attended were Rup's friends. I continued working in the civil hospital and had friends in my husband's circle. We visited my parents regularly.

Time heals; people were getting used to it. In the beginning my husband was careful not to land in a conflict with anyone, especially local people. I am still surprised today to see Meitei girls marrying Mayangs and the weddings being arranged by the girls' parents. It is so different than in the fifties.

My oldest daughter, Lata, was born in Jorhat Mission

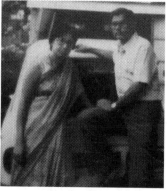

Figure 19 behind our first fiat car 1963

Hospital as Rup started many of his business contacts in Tuli in Nagaland. He had come across some officials who were planning to make a paper mill in Nagaland. I had taken maternity leave from work and we went to Jorhat via Kohima, where he had a very good friend, Gohain. Gohain was from Assam and married a Naga lady who had a daughter from a Meitei husband. After the birth of our daughter, I stayed in their house in Kohima for about a month while Rup was busy with his work.

Rup's supply business was in full swing in Nagaland and Manipur. After we came back to Imphal, my grandmother and mother arranged some Manipuri style gifts of welcome for the baby. My brother Tuleswer regularly picked up the baby's soiled clothes and brought them back washed. By 1963, I resigned from my hospital work as my husband wanted to travel and wanted me to accompany him. Thus, I became a full time housewife.

One day, when we visited my parent's house, my father suggested we build a house in the front, on the empty portion of the plot of land. It had a pond, which needed to be filled up with earth. It was no doubt a very welcome proposal as Rup started earning good income out of his contract business. Ultimately, we built our first dream house on the plot of land at Keishampat. Here is a picture of that house. We had to design it to fit the shape of the land my father gave us. After we finished the ground floor in 1964, we invited my in-laws to come and visit us in Imphal. That was when I was pregnant with my second child. On June 5th 1964, my second baby girl Shobha was born and the first thing they looked for was her complexion. They were very happy that the baby had fair complexion.

My in-laws left after few days for their home in Delhi. Rup was busy with his work and away from home many days at a time. I adjusted my lifestyle accordingly. I did my knitting and embroidery for children and adults with machines and made *more friends. I read lots of books, especially ones authored by Pearl S. Buck. She was my favorite author.*

When my second daughter was about four months old, Rup suggested we all go for a pilgrimage to Amaranth with my parents and his parents. It was a big step. We decided to leave my baby Shobha with my grandmother and an ayah (a maid) while we were away for the pilgrimage. I was a bit hesitant but I knew my grandmother was capable of

Figure 20 With our children Lata, Shobha, Jibesh, Anita

looking after my baby and she would take good care of her. So after some hesitation, I agreed to leave her with my grandma and went to Amarnath, Kashmir for the pilgrimage. When Nehru had tried to reach Amaranth, he couldn't reach the place. It was supposed to have been a very difficult journey during earlier times. But by the time we took the journey, it was not so bad as roads were already made and we had been provided by the government good arrangement so the pilgrims could have a smooth journey.

My parents came to Jammu and then my in-laws, Rup, Lata, who was two and a half also reached Jammu, and we all made the bus journey to the Srinagar valley. At that time, Kashmir was a peaceful place and it was a favorite holiday spot for Indians and foreigners alike. Also most of the Indian movies were shot there. In Kashmir, we stayed on a house boat on Dal Lake for two days and took the city tour. I had seen the pictures of this exquisitely beautiful place in the movies only. But being there in the valley of Srinagar and watching the beautiful snow clad mountains I held my breath. Such a stunningly beautiful place could be only in heaven.

We registered ourselves for the trip to Amarnath Cave along with other five thousand pilgrims. Four porters were engaged for carrying the necessary tents, beddings and foodstuffs for the journey. It was my mother's first journey outside Manipur and Assam whereas my father had gone on other pilgrimages.

The first day of the pilgrimage, we took taxis, driving about 16 km to Pahalgam, a small uniquely enchanting town. We slept the night at Pahalgam and started our journey in the morning after breakfast. The journey to reach the holy cave situated at 14,500 ft above sea level required walking, taking a palki (a chair with two handles held by porters), or riding on horseback. My-in-laws and my mother took the palki and the rest of us rode on horses. Lata was carried by one of the porters.

Our next stop was Chandanwara, the second day. We rested and ate our meals, and then on the third day we reached the top of Pisso, about a 9 km rise. Now most of the paths were covered with snow, and sometimes we had to cross on the connecting bridges formed by the thick layers of snow in between the hills. Most of the time, Rup and I walked along the snow path while the horses and their masters followed us.

Figure 21 On the way to Amarnath Cave, Kashmir

The stillness of the hills and the cool chilly breeze all along the way made me feel as if I were in a forbidden heaven. Pilgrims, old and young, trudged along on the snow-covered paths enduring all the difficulties. I am sure God took pity on us and welcomed us and our souls trying to connect with the Almighty.

We were in Wajau camp at 12000 ft above sea level on the Himalayan Range.

We reached Sheshnag camp on the fourth day, which was about 7.4 miles way from Wajau. The official camps were set up for all the pilgrims. Some arrived early while others reached the camp quite late. Sheshnag Lake was by the side of the camp; we could see the milky water of the lake and snakes swimming. This picture here was at 14000 ft above sea level. On the fifth day, after a six km walk, we reached Panchatarni where five streams meet. Walking was becoming tougher. From Panchatarni we could see the steep climb and the entrance to the cave of Amarnath.

Now everyone had to walk on foot, no horse or carriage allowed. That was the place my in-laws said they did not want to go further. Their health was not good and with her weight, my mother-in-law was finding it extremely difficult to climb uphill.

Since we had come so far, my husband insisted that they should somehow try to reach the top to the cave. They finally agreed, and two porters supported them. In this way, they managed to slowly reach the cave. My mother and father managed to reach the cave without any support. The mythology states that we are supposed to see two doves in the cave, but I don't remember seeing any. Since there were so many people there (the number who registered was 5,000 that year), we had to hurry our prayer and we didn't have time to look out to the Shiv linga of snow (image of lord Shiva of Hindus) and meditate on the Lord. On the downward journey back, we all reached Pahalgam within twenty-four hours. We went to the city of Srinagar and the next day my family and in-laws left for Delhi and my father and mother for Brindaban near Delhi, another holy place for Hindus.

People from Manipur go to many places on pilgrimages but rarely to the Amarnath holy cave. My father and mother were very happy that they made it to such a difficult place to reach and such a mystical place as Amarnath. Later reaching Amarnath Cave became my father's favorite story. I am so happy that my parents could go with us to the Holy Cave.

Yours lovingly,
Ine

*   *   *

Journal Entries
San Ramon, California
January 15, 2009

The miracle on the Hudson River was headline news today. US Airways aircraft, flight 1549, was struck by a flock of Canada Geese during its initial climb at LaGuardia Airport causing the engines to dysfunction. There were 155 passengers aboard, including crew members. Chesley Sullenberger was the captain who executed safely an emergency water landing on the Hudson River saving the lives of the passengers and crew members.

February 14, 2009

I paid $35 as deposit for my book publication to a self-publishing company. That was the silliest thing I ever did. I found out later that there are many more publishing companies ready to publish at much cheaper prices and also many offer more services.

March 5, 2009

Dr. Badar advises me to see an oncologist about my low blood platelet count. So I contact Dr. Shoba Kankipatti, who happened to be Sindhi, the same as my husband's community and we had become more like family. But now I have to change my primary care doctor as I have changed my insurance. That is an important decision at this time. Since I am retired and income is limited I have to be more careful with my expenses.

Journal Entry
San Ramon, California
March 19, 2009

I go to see the flower show at the city's de Young Museum with MaryLou. The Reverend McMillan (Irish) gives a demonstration on flower arrangement. His theme is on a poem "A Coat" by William Butler Yeats. Irish people love poetry.

A Coat

I made my song a coat
Covered with embroideries
Out of old mythologies
From heel to throat
But the fools caught it

Song, let them take it
For there is more enterprise
In walking naked.

We both enjoy the demonstration and the flower arrangement show. This is always going to be a precious memory for me.

*   *   *

March 21, 2009

I volunteer to help feed the homeless with the Seva Dal of Sai organization. I wanted to sign up to volunteer as it is on my birthday.

I cut about a kilo of onions as well as some ingredients like ginger, green pepper, and garlic and refrigerated them so that I can prepare just before going to a Modesto shelter tomorrow. Next day after breakfast, I sautéed the onion and other masalas (spices) in a big pan over high heat. Everything came out well, a blessing of Baba. Sapna and Ravi picked me up at the IHOP parking lot. Lakshmi from Livermore joined us in feeding the homeless. She contributed rice to be served with the bean curry.

Once we arrived at Modesto we got our cooked items out and deposited them at Madhu's place where there was good arrangement for heating the food before feeding people at the Salvation Army Shelter. Before going to the shelter, Madhu and Jayant provided us a Gujarati style lunch. It was delicious. After our service at the center, we came back and reached home around 9:30 pm.

I had submitted a story entitled the "Python under my Grapefruit tree" to the Story Circle Network's journal. It will be my first publication in a journal, dedicated to women writers.

March 22, 2009

At 1:45 pm I attended a chipping clinic at San Ramon Golf Club conducted by Dave Turtle for the Fore Women Golf Association.

March 28, 2009

Jibesh, Colleen, Gavin and Brayden walk in. They have come again from Toronto, Canada without letting me know. A surprise gift for my birthday on 21st March. It is Shobha and Jibesh's decision. Next day we visit Fisherman's Warf and have Clam Chowder for lunch. We take the kids on the Nile Train Ride. It turns out to be an exciting experience for them as the open train ride winds through the sides of the hills crossing over the streams below. The whistling of the train along with the steam emitting is an experience for everyone.

March 30, 2009

Colleen accompanies me to the Walnut Creek SSI office to talk about my social security benefits. Jibesh and his family leave for Toronto on April 1.

* * *

San Ramon, California
October 10, 2002
Dear Gojen,

When I think of those four years during which I had gone to Delhi for my studies, I realize that I didn't know much about what was going at home. Neither was I informed about financial situation. The household was manageable with my father's pay and he didn't have to spend money on me except for the monthly Rs 20.00 (twenty) he paid for my pocket money. Irabanta was about seven years old when I left for Delhi to pursue nursing studies. As usual my father was the tutor for him for school homework. He also had a worse experience than I had. My father's tutoring as usual involved whacking with a ruler and his anger. In the winter Irabanta wore thick woolen cloths so he didn't get hurt much when the ruler came down on him. Eventually, sharing our stories, we'd end up laughing when we recalled our experiences of childhood.

My grandmother's wish to make Irabanta play the role of Lord Krishna in a dance drama known as Rasleela was fulfilled. Playing the role of Lord Krishna was a dedication to Lord Krishna. Meiteis Hindus believed that playing the role of the Lord Krishna was a way to go to heaven and ensure a better life in one's next birth. Since I grew up in Jiribam, my grandmother hadn't had a chance to make me play the role of Radha, consort of Lord Krishna. She always regretted that by the time we moved to Imphal, I was too grown up to play that role. She was therefore determined to make my brother Irabanta play the role while she herself took the role of one of the Gopi's, who were Lord Krishna's devotees. So both Grandmother and Irabanta took part in the dance drama in the local temple hall and at Kaina Hill, a holy place for the Hindu Meities.

Kanya Hill is one of the tourist attractions in Manipur. The present image of Govindaji in the palace was carved from a jackfruit tree in Kanya. There were seven images carved from that tree and installed in different temples at different places in and around Imphal.

The story goes like this: In 1759 AD Rajashri Bhagyachandra became king of Manipur but was defeated in 1765 AD by Hsinbyusin, son of the great Burmese King Alungpaya. He had to flee to Cachar, Assam and took refuge in the court of King Swargadeva Rajeswer Singh of Tekhau. His maternal uncle plotted against him along with the Burmese warriors and wrote to the Assamese king that Bhagyachandra was an imposter. So the King arranged for an encounter between Bhagyachandra and a mad elephant.

As Bhagyachandra was a spiritual person, the night before the encounter, Lord Krishna came into his dream saying that he would be in Kaina as a jackfruit tree and Bhagyachandra was to carve a replica of him to be installed in the Palace Temple. The next day when the mad elephant sent by the king of Assam arrived to confront Bhagyachandra, to everybody's amazement, the elephant bowed in front

Figure 22 grandmother and Irabanta in Rashleela dance drama 1956

of King Bhagyachandra. Ultimately, that was the reason why the Assamese king was ready to help him and thus restored the kingdom of Manipur to him.

Once he was restored to the kingship, Bhagyachandra Maharaja became so busy with the affairs of his kingdom that he forgot about the jackfruit tree. He was reminded of it in the form of a little boy loitering around the hill and asking for food from a village woman. The old woman from the hill became curious and wanted to know his identity. The boy at last disclosed to her who he was. After that day the boy was never seen.

The King came to know about the incident and with the help of his advisors sent some of his people to look for the tree. When the first axe fell on it, blood oozed out and had to be stopped. Only after worshipping with a ritual by a priest it was decided that the roots of the tree would be uprooted and the whole tree brought down the river to Langthaband. After the wood was dried completely, carvings of images were begun. The first one was brought to Govindaji for the temple of Imphal palace. The second was brought to Bihoynath Govinda at Sagolband, and a third was for Shree Gopinath at Ningthoukhong. The fourth was for Shree Nityananda (Arambam Nityananda) at Khwai lamabam leikai, Imphal. A fifth was for Shree Madanmohan at Oinam Thingel, Imphal. The sixth was Anuprabhu of Nabadwip at Nadia of West Bengal. And the seventh and last sculpture, which was finished from the root of the tree and installed in Lamangdong, was known as Advaita Prabhu or Lamangdong Advaita.

The site of the sacred jackfruit tree at Kaina was declared an historical archaeological site of Manipur and the Government set up a center to attract tourists.

The picture above is of one of the dance dramas known as Rash Leela performed by my grandmother Sana Chaubi as one of the Gopi's and my brother Irabanta as lord Krishna.

Irabanta passed his matriculation examination in 1963 and attended college for two years in science. Then in 1966, we decided to send him to Delhi for premedical courses in one of the privately run colleges. Since Hindi is a national language, it was compulsory to pass for entering the premedical course. That *became a problem for Irabanta, and he came back to Imphal to complete his degree course in science. Later he joined Rup in starting a supply business to government offices. He learned fast and ultimately, established his own successful business.*

When I started working, I was interested in helping Tuleswer, the younger of the two brothers (you'll remember that he was born on Nov 23rd 1951 and when he was only a few months old, his birth mother Tamphasana passed away leaving him under the care of my mother) go to a good school and so put him in the Little Flower School. I very much wanted him to become a well-educated human being. But by the time he was in sixth grade, he fell in with bad company, and instead of attending school, he spent his days playing elsewhere and came back home each day at the end of school hours. Father had also stopped tutoring him so he didn't know how behind he was in his studies. In seventh grade, he got admission and started to attend Chingmeirong High school but wasn't able to keep up with the classes. Again he fell into bad company. The school staff advised him to study privately. He could pass his matriculation examination privately.

All my ambitions and hopes were shattered when he eloped with a girl when he was just 18 and the girl just 16. Without any regular income, he was married and had three sons. Eventually, Rup took him to Tuli to work at the paper mill construction site and he was given charge of looking after the vehicles and transportation of the staff. His three sons were doing well in the local school in Tulli. After two years, he returned to Imphal and depended mostly on my mother's pension. He was again blessed with another son and a cute daughter.

He had lots of talents but couldn't utilize them properly to earn a living. He succumbed to drinking. His life was cut short with his health problems when he died on August 5, 2002. Life turns out sometimes the opposite of what we want. God bless his soul. My brother Tuleswer was always available when we needed him; he was a good human being. I am glad to know his children are all doing well.

Yours Lovingly,
Ine

*   *   *

Journal Entry
April 4, 2009

I get an email message from Gojen, who lives in Imphal, India, about their new insurance business. They seem to be doing well.

May 10, 2009

Now only a few days later, I come to know that Gojen and his wife's insurance business turns out to be a mishap. They are victims of a scam with a heavy price to pay

Journal Entries
San Ramon, California
April 18, 2009

I start my online class with Matilda for writing memoir and I am working more on using the five senses in my writing. I had my class conference call with Matilda and Kendra Bonnet along with other students.

April 20, 2009

I had my first appointment with Axis community; they needed my medical history, which Dr. Badar sent.

April 26, 2009

I had a dentist appointment with Dr. Tirupathi Haritha on Alcosta Blvd in Dublin. The tooth Dr. Dimayuga advised be extracted was just filled on May 11th. It is still doing well and that surprises me. Good that I didn't go for the extraction of the tooth.

May 5, 2009

It is a very challenging day as I left my cell phone at Pangila's place the day before. I am supposed to receive Mahlo and her daughter Dolly at the Dublin Bart station. They are waiting for me on the Pleasanton side of the station while I am on the Dublin side waiting for them. I walk up and down looking for them. After waiting for about 45 minutes, I drive home and call my friend Pangila. I come to know that since they haven't seen me, they take a taxi to Freemont and Rupinder, Pangila's son, picks them up. I feel awful about this incident. The previous day I should have gone back to get my cell phone then things would have been different.

May 6, 2009

I join a trip to Saratoga, sponsored by the Senior Center. The tour of the Hakone Japanese garden is something I will remember always. The tour of downtown Saratoga brings back nostalgic moments. Somehow downtown Saratoga reminds me of the day walking with my husband in the streets of London and Paris 35 years back.

June 27, 2009

I am into my writing and golf at the same time. I have been playing with the Emerging Golf Group, a part of the Fore Women Golf Association. Many of the members prefer to remain with this group, EGG.

The next day I receive an offer from a neighbor to become a caregiver for her mother, Mary Miller, who was a customer when I was working as a hairstylist for JC Penney, and later, we met again in a poetry writing group. The offer was tempting, but I don't want to be tied down as I have lots of things on my plate.

I am grateful that I have friends like Barbara and Mary Lou, who are regulars with me at our coffee place and with whom I see movies. Sana from Manipur and Pangila from Nagaland, a neighboring state in India, are my closest friends, but we could meet only once a while as we live quite far away from each other. Neither drives and I am the only one who can drive and meet them. But the telephone is a good way to communicate and I am grateful for that.

July 12, 2009

I attend Sunday Bhajan at Ishani's place in Livermore wearing my blue siffon (a kind of soft silk sari). I feel good when I get a complement from my daughter. But I don't feel comfortable these days wearing Indian dress. I believe the saying, "While in Rome do as the Romans do."

*   *   *

San Ramon, California
December 14, 2003

Dear Gojen,

While we were living in Shillong in 1974, I got a call from Imphal.

"Mummy, it is a call from Imphal." My daughter Lata handed the phone to me. It must be from my brother Irabanta as no one else was there to call me, I thought to myself. I grabbed the phone and I had a kind of weird feeling.

"Hello," I said.

"It is me,"

When there was news, my brother wanted to convey, he called me, otherwise we did not talk much on phone in those

Figure 23 My father Ibungohal Singh 1950

days. We had to book the call through an operator and get the connections with the other end.

"Pabung's condition is very serious."

"What's happened?"

"He looked all right when I saw him the last time only two months ago."

I learned that my father had become semi-conscious and delirious.

Luckily my husband Rup was home after a month's tour for his work, and I told him I needed to leave for Imphal immediately.

When I reached Imphal, my mother looked really worried and was sitting by Father's bedside. I walked in and stood near him. His eyes were closed and he was breathing normally. His face, though, was pale and thin, and he was not aware of the surroundings.

"Pabung," I called to him. He did not answer. He seemed not at all conscious of my arrival. Sometimes, though, he mumbled a few words. I was not sure what he wanted to say. I couldn't believe a commanding figure of the family like my father was lying like a helpless baby. The visiting doctor had started him on a glucose drip for nourishment as he was not eating anything. All of our close relatives were informed. Radhapyari and her husband Kumar, who was a doctor, was there looking after my father. I was in doubt that Father would survive another week. Radhapyari and her husband stayed overnight the third day of my arrival. I did not see any signs of improvement in my father's condition. His condition was declining, and whenever doctors gave him Coramin injections to improve his heart beat, he started mumbling, "Don't block my way, let me go." My father was ready.

We could all see my father slowly taking breath with long intervals. The time had come to call the local maiba to perform a last rights ritual. It was with emotional turmoil that I saw my father's last slow, labored breaths while his soul was leaving his mortal body.

Father's body was covered with a white sheet. According to Meitei Manipuri custom, a lifeless body cannot be kept inside the house, so he was placed soon in our front yard near a tulsi plant awaiting cremation. As it was monsoon season, he was soaked with pouring rain. This sight made me very sad. But some said it was a message of blessings from heaven that he was cleaned before God took him to heaven. What I know is that my father was at peace when he left us forever on June 5th, 1974.

Yours lovingly,
Ine

*   *   *

Journal Entries
San Ramon, California
August 13, 2009

My friends Pangila and Sana come over to my place to stay for two nights. Pangila's son Rupinder after dropping them leaves for San Jose. We spend time shopping in the stores around my place, and then cook, eat, and watch films on TV. After two days, Sana's daughter Olivia comes to pick them up. Being together is enjoyable but a bit tiring at the end, though. Age is showing now.

August 18, 2009

I attend the creative writing and water color painting classes for seniors offered by Las Positas college at the Dublin Senior Center. At first, there was a big crowd in the writing class, and I felt nervous to read in front of such a big crowd. But after some weeks, the number of attendees thinned out. The teacher is new to the group and the students are continuing from the previous session. But by the next session the enrollment is so low that the center does not offer the classes. I join another program at the San Ramon Senior Center.

August 22, 2009

Tonight there is a dinner party at our house for family friends Sarat, Ginnie and their kids, Rahul, Avika, and another family, Ramki, Manju and their daughter Nini. Shobha's school friend Paro and her husband Sujan came along, too, with their kids Shrey and Dhruv. I make some special dishes for the party. Sarat's mom Saroj and Paro's mom Seva, are also among the group. I am happy that I have some senior ladies for company.

September 2, 2009

Still working on my memoir and on some vignettes. I've submitted a short memoir to Story Circle Network journal. They will publish my second short memoir in the journal this year. Only when I start taking classes on line from Matilda, the author of *Rosie* I take my writing more seriously and continue to write.

September 16, 2009

My grandsons, Lucas and Leon who are twins, celebrate their 17th birthday today. I get gift cards for them from Yogurt Place.

September 18, 2009

We went to Sycamore Grove Park to do landscape painting. I am continuing with my online class for coral painting but I don't enjoy it because there is too much technical involvement. The painting with coral technique is fully computerized and I get confused. So I don't enjoy doing this anymore. Lucas helps me create a blog, *JDA's Creative Moments*.

November 7, 2009

Visited an interesting exhibit at the Academy of Science exhibition hosted by IBM.

November 9, 2009

Today is the anniversary of the fall of the Berlin wall, 20 years back. It took days and weeks to dismantle it.

*   *   *

San Ramon, California
July 20, 2004

Dear Gojen,

    It was first week of March 2003, when Irabanta called. In his usual positive tone, he said, "Gojen's wedding is going to be on the 30th March. You have to come for the wedding."

Figure 24 Wedding of Gojen and Ranjeeta March 30,2003

    I couldn't believe it. Your mother, Shanti, my sister-in-law, was seriously ill and was in her sick bed due to advanced case of cancer. I couldn't believe a wedding for their only son was planned. I came to know that your mother wanted to see you get married and take care of their household, as she knew that she wouldn't be alive much longer. She was only in her early fifties.

    "Who is the girl?"

    "The girl is from Moirang. She is related tof the ex-chief minister of Manipur, Koireng Singh."

    In spite of my sister-in-law's health, I was happy at hearing the news of your wedding coming up so soon. With excitement, I conveyed the news to my daughter Shobha. I took leave from JCPenney and booked my ticket for the flight to New Delhi on Russian Airlines to arrive there a week before the wedding. After spending two days at my sister-in-law Raj's house, I took a flight to Imphal. I could not believe my eyes when I saw the condition of Shanti, who had become helpless and very weak. It was unbearable to watch her breathe as she was in such pain. She was given the strongest sedative, and even that didn't work for her.

"Shanti, I am here." I sat down beside her.

She opened her eyes and saw me but she could not say a word and closed her eyes again. Then the pain came back as if a knife were slowly piercing her flesh; she could do nothing to stop it. She had been one who took care of us all and now she lay helpless and in pain. I couldn't help but pray for an end to her suffering.

I missed the olden times when Shanti and I confided in each other and spent time chatting. She gave me all the news of our relatives and told me about your troubled life, Gojen. I am so happy to see you in good health and in your present life condition. The anxieties and worries your parents had to endure! I am grateful to God, you are a shining star now. Also I thank God that you married a smart, educated and beautiful girl.

Figure 25 Gojen's mother Shanti earlier days dressed up for a social event.

Knowing her life was soon going to be over, your mother managed to get some of her relatives to introduce to you to Ranjeeta from Moirang town. Elopement was an acceptable system in our Meitei society. As I told you in the story about my grandfather, the girl is usually kept in at one of her friend's house for the night and the next day her parents are informed of the elopement by a group of elderly men from the neighborhood. If everything goes well, arrangements for the wedding are discussed and finalized and a date is set. Ranjeeta's parents accepted the proposal and set your wedding date. Ranjeeta would stay at her parents' house until the wedding day.

Shanti's older sister took the place of the groom's mother on Sunday the 30th of March 2003. It was a very sad moment for Shanti as she couldn't attend the wedding of her only son. But at the same time, her consolation was that her son was marrying and her daughter-in-law would be in her house. Yours was the first wedding I attended in Imphal for many years.

The wedding ceremony was noteworthy. Your father had a big friends circle and so many were invited that there was a long procession of cars from Imphal to Moirang, about a one and half hour drive.

As a part of the groom's party, I rode in one of the several cars driven by friends who had volunteered. Buses were rented for the party band and other guests. It was very memorable event, Gojen. I still remember each and every detail of your wedding, when the marriage ritual was performed by the priest and the special person was there by your side to attend you. You were wrapped up in all the cotton shawls as desired by the customs of the Meities. I wondered how you must have felt with the white dhoti and the wide white cotton innaphi wrapped around you and a topi (turban) tied on your head. I remarked on how the bride was decorated, but the groom was dressed so simply. You were instructed to sit on a stool in the center of the mandap (hall) where all the invitees sat circle around you watching the ceremony ritual performed by the priest.

After a while the bride was escorted from the house dressed up in a potloi (bridal dress) and shining decorative hair pieces. She was led by a woman and all of her relatives followed in a procession until she reached the middle of the mandap (hall) and was seated next to you, the groom

The priest performed the rituals with coconut, flowers and sindur (the red powder to be put on the forehead). Then you and your bride exchanged garlands of flowers. Afterward, the bride was made to walk in a circle seven times and at every round she completed, armfuls of flowers were offered to the groom signaling that the groom was now her Lord. This custom is slightly different from in the rest of India because in Northern Indian custom, the bride and the groom together go around the fire seven times. And in our custom we don't use the fire. Once the ritual was complete, both of you, bowed to Ranjeeta's parents and grandparents, uncles and aunts to receive their blessing.

After you were blessed as a couple, your bride was taken to your home in a long procession of cars led by a bus with a band's party music. In olden days, the bride was usually taken to her groom's home in a Dolai (a decorated carrier with handles usually made of wood and carried by four men). Alternately, the bride was taken on an elephant and threw coins on the way. That was the sign of a wealthy family. Those carriers of Dolai with bride used to get lots of money after they completed their journey.

Figure 26 Olivia dressed in mordern Manipuri Meitei style.

After five days of the wedding, the bride's parents hosted the Chak-kauba, a customary lunch given to all the friends and relatives of the groom and bride. Your in-laws were informed that about 200 guests would be attending the luncheon party from your side.

Manipuri woman usually dresses like the one in the picture. 21st century women of Manipur have changed the dress styles quite a lot from what they were in the olden days but still we can see the traditional style.

Here is the picture of a modern Manipuri Meitei dressed in Manipuri Meitei style for a social event. (Model Oliva khuraijam.) The picture is a model of how a modern Manipuri girl is decked up in gold jewelry and a colorful phanek /skirt and innaphi/scarf both created by local artists and weavers. The intricate design of gold jewelry is made by the local Meitei craftsmen who specialize in this art. The original Manipuri gold necklace, the Marai, is the valued possession of a woman. I enclose this picture and the description of your wedding to let my friends from other nationalities know about our Manipuri Meitei culture and traditions as well as to insure there is a record for future generations of how your wedding was performed.

Yours lovingly,
Ine

*   *   *

Journal Entries
San Ramon, California
January 1, 2010

The new year starts with a bhajan (prayer song) at Swapna's place going from 10 pm to 12 am. I give Swapna a box of chocolates and a candle holder as New Year's gifts. The Bhajan ends with snacks and fruit, and when I reach home it is 1 am. Surprisingly, Shobha and Lall are watching a Hindi movie and we wish each other a happy new year. In the morning around 10 am we all go to the Livermore Hindu Temple to celebrate the new year. There is a long line as usual and it takes us about an hour to get inside the temple for worshipping.

January 3, 2010

Shobha, Lall and I went to the housewarming of Vijaya, who worked at Wells Fargo Bank. As I had my shawl folded in hand, my daughter remarked that shawl wouldn't be necessary. Still I decided to take it with me. Once we reached Pittsburg, it was cloudy and foggy. Luckily, my daughter had her jacket in the trunk and was protected from the cold. Mostly South Indian families attended. Lots of snacks and also lunch with a variety of dishes served.

*　　*　　*

San Ramon, California
March 10, 2007
Dear Gojen,

After my retirement in 2006, I decided to visit all my relatives in India. I made my itinerary for Delhi, Poona, Mumbai, Bangalore, Tirpatti, Puttapurthi, then last to my hometown Imphal. I planned for two months' vacation and spent one of them visiting my husband's relatives in Pune, Bangalore, and Mumbai. I flew back to Delhi and stayed with my sister-in-law Raj Gandhi. After two days, I flew to Imphal via Guwahati. At the Imphal airport, you were waiting for me, and seeing everyone at Keishampat, I felt as if I were also being welcomed by my deceased parents.

Irabanta already had some plans for me. There was a wedding coming up at Cachar. Imashi Tamphasana, Irabanta and Tuleswer's birth mother, who you will remember came to our house as a young bride for our father (arranged by my grandmother), had one sister in Cachar whose grandson was getting married in a week. We purchased our air tickets for Guwahati where the wedding ceremony was to take place.

Unfortunately, I started having swelling of my right knee and was in acute pain during that time. Still I decided to attend the wedding with Irabanta and travelled with the help of a pain killer.

While in Guwahati, I stayed with Hazarikas, our old neighbor when we lived in Shillong, a beautiful hill town, capital of Megahalaya State of India during the 80s. Mr. and Mrs. Hazarika came down from Shillong specially to see me. It was a precious time being with my old friend for a night at her place at Guwahati (as she had second home there (and at the same time being able to attend the wedding next day.

The wedding was held in Gurudwara at a temple for Sikhs at Guwahati as the bride belonged to Sikh community. I managed to remain at the ceremony, though I had great difficulty sitting down on the carpeted floor along with the groom's party. After the wedding, the groom's party from Cachar lined up in different cars to go back to Cachar where the groom's parents lived. I was given a ride in the same car with the groom and bride along with the boy's mother. I sat in front seat of the car while the bride Rupjyoti and groom Amarjeet sat in the back seat along with groom's mother, Sobha. Their house was at Phuleter, Konjem leikai, Cachar. Their building looked magnificent amidst the plain huts and houses of the village. It had accommodations for all her four sons with bedrooms and living rooms attached and fully furnished.

When the groom's party reached Cachar, the priest of that community had to sanctify the wedding with rituals because the bride was not from the Meitei community, and she would not be able to take part in Meitei's society unless the priest had sanctified her. The parents had organized the ritual, and the girl was accepted by the community priest who was then satisfied with a Dakshina, a money or in-kind offering. The feast usually performed by the bride's family on the fifth day according to custom was performed on the second day at the groom's house. Then everyone was free to leave.

On March 10th, Irabanta and I planned to visit our half-sister Sorojini, at Jiribam. Our host offered us a car and a driver who was very helpful and ready to take us anywhere we wanted to go. We reached Jiribam within half an hour. I did not even realize that we already crossed the bridge on the Jiri River, which we used to cross on small boat when I was a child.

The driver turned toward Dibong and after passing many houses, we couldn't locate Sorojini's house. We saw a roadside stall and stopped there to enquire about the location of Sorojini's house.

"Oh, you have come ahead. Please go back and after five houses, you will see a red gate at the left. That's their house."

We thanked him, instructed the driver to turn the car back and to drive slowly. Then we saw the red

Figure 27 Our half-sister Sorojini and family

gate. "Please stop, we are at the right place," Irabanta instructed the driver.

The driver stopped the car and we got out of it and Irabanta proceeded toward the gate. I followed him. We saw our brother-in-law Mohan sitting in a chair in the front yard basking in the sun. He really looked frail and old. Sorojini came out of the house and stood on the front verandah, the usual place to welcome guests. We stepped onto the verandah and Sorojini hugged me and started crying. Tears of joy, I hope. I was seeing her after at least four decades.

"We are happy to see each other; why cry?" I consoled her. We three stood there, all three of us from one father but different mothers. A beautiful family reunion. She had been waiting with lunch already made for us. But before we had started out, we had had breakfast cum lunch at Sobha's house. "How can you do that?" she scolded us. "I have prepared our food. You have to have lunch with us," she insisted.

I really felt bad and told Irabanta we had to eat again. So we both said we would have a little lunch.

Sorojini went to the kitchen to finish cooking, and while we waited for her, we talked with Mohan, who was not able to hear us properly. We had to almost shout so that he could hear us. The conversation was not a smooth one. At last after about thirty minutes, Sorojini said lunch was ready. Due to my knee problem, I could not sit on the floor and eat as was the custom. So she made us sit on the mura and then on the side table for eating our lunch was served. Rice, fish curry, and iIronba (a special side dish like pickle with lots of hot pepper), it was sumptuous, so we had a full meal for the second time.

Sorojini also finished her lunch and got ready to take us to the villages and also the place where our quarter had been. After my father was transferred, Mohan, Sorojini's husband was appointed as administrative assistant in place of father. He and Sorojini then stayed in the same quarter where we used to live. She also referred to the grapefruit tree and she had kept seedlings from the same tree, which I now saw growing in her back yard. But the shape of my original grapefruit was not there in its seedlings.

When we reached the place where our quarter used to be, I was shocked. I could not recognize the place. I couldn't even locate where our house had been. I could not figure out where my favorite grapefruit tree was. The beautiful green field was occupied with different buildings and the pond was no longer there. Instead a huge building had been built for shopping complex. Most painful, really, was that my grapefruit tree was no longer there, but I felt the roots deep down under the ground wanting to greet me. The sweet memories of my childhood place will remain deep in my heart forever even though the area is now filled with modern constructions and development. The most surprising thing was that the villages in Jiribam and Cachar had remained the same as when I'd seen them as a child. Only Babupara and neighboring areas were completely transformed and overcrowded.

Sorojini's two married daughters, who were living in Jiribam, came to see us. They were very excited to see us as we had not met before. It was the time of holi, the festival of color, and I gave Rs. 100 to the kids. We bid farewell to my dear Sorojini and her family and came back to Konjeng Leikai where the newly married couple was living. We stayed the night and returned to Imphal on a flight from Silchar airport.

Yours lovingly,
Ine

*   *   *

Journal Entries
San Ramon, CA
January 11, 2010

I am still going on with my painting project, and, even though I need to spend money from my limited income, I continue to do it as it keeps me in a positive mindset, which contributes to my health.

Today I feel a bad hair day and decide to give my hair random highlights.

January 13, 2010

The Senior Center tour to Sea Elephant was postponed. On the way, there was funny noise coming from the bus. After some time, the driver diverted the bus to a shopping plaza in Foster City, and we were informed that a new bus would be coming to pick us up and take us back to the Senior Center; a new date for the tour would be decided later on.

Rupinder is leaving for LA soon and has asked me if I can pick up his mother Pangila and spend some days with her until he comes back.

January 14, 2010

We celebrate Lall's 48th birthday with a cake made by my grandson Lucas.

January 15, 2010

I pick up Pangila give her my room and bed while I take Dev's bed as he is out of town.

January 16, 2010

Shobha, Lall, and Lucas leave for Frankfurt to see Mala's performance. They will have a good time there even though it is quite cold. I usually attend church once a year during Christmas or New Year's, so Pangila and I go to a church to greet the new year. Rupinder comes to our house and after having dinner, he drives back to his home in San Jose with his mom.

January 20, 2010

MaryLou is at my house to plan for our chapbook project and then lunch at Maxi's.

In the evening Shobha, Lall, and Lucas return from Europe. I am glad to see the video of Mala's program "India" in Frankfurt.

The classes sponsored by Las Positas College for watercolor painting were not filling well and the next session is cancelled. I joined a class in Chinese brush painting, which has now become my favorite subject.

MaryLou and I had been trying to pick among our poems and combine them into a book. I had given her my poems to read and a material for a Table of Contents. But she had not shown her poems to me. How were we going to publish together if she didn't want to show her poems to me? I decided to opt out of our plan and have my poems edited by Lorraine Mej-Green, my online teacher from Story Circle Network. Then I publish my first poetry book, *Land of the Dancing Deer*, before the end of 2010 though Lulu.com

February 4, 2010

I leave for the Story Circle Network conference in Austin. Meeting my memoir writing teacher, Linda Joy Myers, at the Oakland airport is very exciting. We hug each other before boarding together for Austin. At the conference,

Story Circle members are very helpful. When they see someone alone they make sure to ask to join them.

February 7, 2010

I return home energized and resume my usual painting and writing along with golf. Dev is still home and I hand him a birthday gift of $50 before he leaves for college at Chapman University in Southern California.

Manipuri group in the Bay Area celebrates the Hindu holi festival of color at Olivia and Sudeep's place. Because of our Manipuri social group here, we no longer miss the festivals at home.

March 24, 2010

My son Jibesh calls me and gives the most unbelievable news. He and Colleen are definitely in the process of separation. I am in shock. Shobha and Lall also are quite surprised. Jibesh and Colleen have been having some problems for the last year we presume. Even though we felt something was not right we never imagined it would end up like this. Colleen is no longer in love with my son Jibesh and that is the reason why she wants a divorce. So we all take flight to Washington DC where my nephew and niece live. Jibesh also comes over to meet us. We are there to give him moral support. After we spend the week together we all head back to our own destinations.

We get the news from Jibesh that they are preparing the boys, talking to them about their parents' decision and letting them know the arrangement. The boys, who are eight and six, are upset and start crying but will gradually adjust. The boys are to be with their mother whereas on alternate weekends and every Wednesday, their father will have them. He will also pay child support. They have just sold their townhouse and now live separately in their own apartments.

*   *   *

San Ramon, California
January 2, 2010
Dear Gojen,

It was 3 am here in California when I got a call from you on December 23ʳᵈ, 2009. I sensed something was not right because no one calls at this time.

"Hello Aunty."

"Yes Gojen, what is the news?" Is there something, some bad news or what? You wouldn't be calling me at this hour? He gave the phone to his father to talk to me.

"Talk to Pabung," he said and I waited for Irabanta's voice.

"Ichemma, we are at Pabungcha's house. He passed away a few hours ago and we are here for his cremation."

I could not believe my ears. He was my father's first cousin as the grandfathers were siblings. He was the only living person from whom I could get information about our ancestors. Now I don't have anyone from whom

Figure 28
uncle Chandrahas

I can learn about the history of our ancestors. Exactly one year back, I saw him and talked to him. He was very happy to see me, and though he was confined and could not walk around, he was mentally alert.

"Don't worry, my father lived well past 90 and I will also be here."

But it didn't happen that way and he passed away on December 23rd, 2009, one year short of 90. Our beloved Uncle Chandrahas will be remembered always.

Gojen, I want to let you know that whatever I have written so far is a record of our ancestors including Manipuri Meitei customs and traditions prevalent during the days when I grew up. It is a record for future generations of our family so that they will have knowledge about their ancestors, and it is also a record of the times in our part of India during the 1940s and 50s. Though some of the customs in the rest of India may be similar, I refer only to those of our community of Meities, as I experienced them. I see the changes taking place in this part of India at such a profound speed now and want to be sure you know how things were before your generation and generations to come.

I remind myself every day that when you grow old, it not merely a loss of youth. Aging is a completion of life's journey (I am paraphrasing Reverend Barbara Smith). Writing to you, my dear nephew, is a big part of completing my journey.

Yours lovingly,
Ine

*   *   *

FAMILY TREE:
MAIBAM SAGEI/ SUBCASTE

Mr. Luwanba married Princess Chingoisana (daughter of King Narasinha of Manipur 1844-1850)
Children:
Mr.Ibungohal   Mr.Iboyyaima   Mr. Tomchou   Miss Tampha

Mr.Tomchou Married Ms Leinau Devi
Children:
Mr. Ibungohal   Mr. Iboyaima   Mr. Kulabisdhu   Ms Pashot

Mr.Ibungohal married Ms Chingnangkhonbi, Ms Ibemhal, Ms Tamphasana
Children:
Ms Sorojini, Ms Jamuna, Mr. Irabanta, Mr.Tuleswer.

Mr.Iboyaima married Ms Rashmi
Children:
Ms Mani

Mr.Kulabidhu married Ms Ramani
Children:
Mr.Jogeshwer, Mr. Ibochou

Ms Pashot married Mr.Kamini
Children: Mr.Jatindra, Ms Radhapyari, (Ms Purnimashi and Mr.Amubi from previous marriage)

Mr.Irabanta married Ms Shanti
Children:
Mr.Gojen

Mr.Tuleshwar married Ms Thoibi
Children:
Mr.Kuki/Doren, Mr. Biren, Mr. Bobbi/Khogen, Mr.Sanatombi, Miss Jharna

Mr.Gojen married Ms. Ranjeeta
Children:
Master Heale, Master Prince

Mr. Doren married Ms Bimola
Children:
Miss Sabrina, and Miss Sally

Mr. Biren married Ms Ashalata /Pita
Children:
Master Roshan

*　　*　　*

MEANING OF OUR MEITEI DIALECTS:

<u>(As taught by my grandmother)</u>

Indon—aunt (mother's side)
Ine—aunt from father's side
Khura—uncle younger than father
Ipael—uncle older than father
Pabung—father (who is a descendent of RK family.)
Pajee—father
Ima—mother-
Imashi—mother (used for RK family)
Iche—elder sister
Ichemma—elder sister for descendents from RK family
Tamo-elder brother who is descendent from RK family
Tada—elder brother for common people
Yambung—elder brother who is of RK.
Abok—grandmother
Aigyabok—grandmother who has title RK.
Ipubok—grandfather
Idhou—grandfather for descendents of RK family
Lai haraoba—god's celebrations of happiness
Sumang—front yard (in the front)

*   *   *

ABOUT THE AUTHOR

 Jamuna Devi Advani is a graduate from Rajkumari Amrit Kaur College of Nursing, University of Delhi, India. She is a voracious reader and is always ready to learn something new in life. She contributes her poems and short memoirs to the Story Circle Network, California Writers Club Journal and Tri-Valley Writers Club anthologies. She is the author of the poetry books *Land of the Dancing Deer* and *Symphony of Heart Songs*. She is an active member of the Danville Poets Society and the Creative Writers Group of the Alcosta

Senior and Community Center, San Ramon CA.